FREE **VIDEO** EXPLANATIONS

MW01617381

GRADE **3**

ARGOPREP
COMMON CORE

READING
COMPREHENSION

MULTIPLE CHOICE WORKBOOK

Authors: Michael Heyman
Anayet Chowdhury
Eduard Suleyman
Vladislav Suleyman

Design: Vladislav Suleyman

At ArgoPrep, we are dedicated to providing quality and effective supplemental practice for your child. We would love to hear your honest feedback and **review** of our workbooks on **Amazon**.

ArgoPrep is one of the leading providers of supplemental educational products and services. We offer affordable and effective test prep solutions to educators, parents and students. Learning should be fun and easy! For that reason, most of our workbooks come with detailed video answer explanations taught by one of our fabulous instructors. Our goal is to make your life easier, so let us know how we can help you by e-mailing us at **info@argoprep.com**

ARGOPREP

OTHER BOOKS BY ARGO BROTHERS

Here are some other test prep workbooks by ArgoPrep you may be interested in. All of our workbooks come equipped with detailed video explanations to make your learning experience a breeze! Subscribe to our mailing list at www.argobrothers.com to receive custom updates about your education.

GRADE 2

GRADE 3

GRADE 4

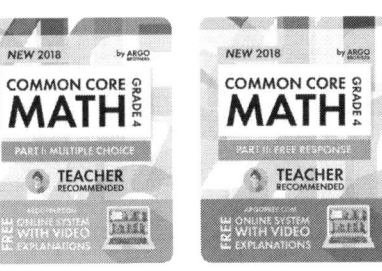

GRADE 5

GRADE 6

GRADE 7

GRADE 3

GRADE 4

TABLE OF
CONTENTS

HOW TO USE THE BOOK

This workbook is designed to give lots of practice with the English Common Core State Standards (CCSS). By practicing and mastering this entire workbook, your child will become very familiar and comfortable with the state english exam. If you are a teacher using this workbook for your student's, you will notice each question is labeled with the specific standard so you can easily assign your students problems in the workbook. This workbook takes the CCSS and divides them up among 20 weeks. By working on these problems on a daily basis, students will be able to (1) find any deficiencies in their understanding and/or practice of english and (2) have small successes each day that will build proficiency and confidence in their abilities.

You can find detailed video explanations to each problem in the book by visiting:
www.argoprep.com

We strongly recommend watching the videos as it will reinforce the fundamental concepts. Please note, scrap paper may be necessary while using this workbook so that the student has sufficient space to show their work.

WEEK 1

VIDEO
EXPLANATIONS

ARGOPREP.COM

Find detailed video explanations to each problem on:
ArgoPrep.com

Rumpelstiltskin

1. Once there was a miller who was poor, but who had a beautiful daughter. Now it happened that he had to go and speak to the King, and in order to make himself appear important he said to him, "I have a daughter who can spin straw into gold."

2. The King said to the miller, "That is an art which pleases me well; if your daughter is as clever as you say, bring her tomorrow to my palace, and I will try what she can do."

3. And when the girl was brought to him he took her into a room which was quite full of straw, gave her a spinning-wheel and a reel, and said, "Now set to work, and if by tomorrow morning early you have not spun this straw into gold during the night, you must die."

4. Suddenly he locked up the room, and left her in it alone. So there sat the poor miller's daughter, and for her life could not tell what to do; she had no idea how straw could be spun into gold, and she grew more and more miserable, until at last she began to weep.

5. But all at once the door opened, and in came a little man, and said, "Good evening, Mistress Miller; why are you crying so?"

6. "Alas!" answered the girl, "I have to spin straw into gold, and I do not know how to do it."

7. "What will you give me," said the little man "if I do it for you?"

8. "My necklace," said the girl.

9. The little man took the necklace, seated himself in front of the wheel, and "whirr, whirr, whirr," three turns, and the reel was full; then he put more straw on, and whirr, whirr, whirr, three times around, and the second reel was full too.

10. And so it went on until the morning, when all the straw was spun, and all the reels were full of gold.

11. By daybreak the King was already there, and when he saw the gold he was astonished and delighted, but his heart became only more greedy. He had the miller's daughter taken into another room full of straw, which was much larger, and commanded her to spin everything in one night again if she valued her life.

11. The girl knew not how to help herself, and was crying, when the door again opened, and the little man appeared, and said, "What will you give me if I spin the straw into gold for you?" "The ring on my finger," answered the girl. The little man took the ring, again began to turn the wheel, and by morning had spun all the straw into glittering gold.

12. The King rejoiced beyond measure at the sight, but still he did not think he had enough gold. The king had the miller's daughter taken into a still larger room full of straw, and said, "You must spin this, too, in the course of this night; but if you succeed, you shall be my wife." "Even if she be a miller's daughter," thought he, "I could not find a richer wife in the whole world."

13. When the girl was alone the little man came again for the third time, and said, "What will you give me if I spin the straw for you this time also?"

14. "I have nothing left that I could give," answered the girl.

15. "Then promise me, if you should become Queen, your first child."

16. "Who knows whether that will ever happen?" thought the miller's daughter; and, not knowing how else to help herself in this crisis, she promised the little man what he wanted, and for that he once more span the straw into gold.

Preview the questions before reading the passage. Circle or underline any key information that will help you.

17. And when the King came in the morning, and found all as he had wished, he took her in marriage, and the pretty miller's daughter became a Queen.
18. A year after, she had a beautiful child, and she never gave a thought of the little man. But suddenly he came into her room, and said, "Now give me what you promised."
19. The Queen was horror-struck, and offered him all the riches of the kingdom if he would leave her the child. But the little man said, "No, something that is living is dearer to me than all the treasures in the world."
20. Then the Queen began to weep and cry, so that the little man felt bad for her. "I will give you three days' time," said he; "if by that time you can find out my name, then you shall you keep your child."
21. So the Queen thought the whole night of all the names that she had ever heard, and she sent a messenger over the country to ask, far and wide, for any other names that there might be.
22. When the little man came the next day, she began with Caspar, Malichi, Brady, and said all the names she knew, one after another; but to every one the little man said, "That is not my name."
23. On the second day she asked everyone in the neighborhood their names, and she repeated to the little man the most uncommon and curious names she heard.
24. "Perhaps your name is Shortribs, or Sheepshanks, or Laceleg?" but he always answered, "That is not my name."
26. On the third day the messenger came back again, and said, "I have not been able to find a single new name, but as I came to a high mountain at the end of the forest, where the fox and the hare said goodnight to each other, there I saw a little house, and before the house there was a fire burning, and around about the fire there was quite a ridiculous little man was jumping: he hopped upon one leg, and shouted --
27. "'Today I bake, tomorrow stew,
   The next I'll have the young Queen's child.
   Ha! glad am I that no one knew
   That Rumpelstiltskin I am styled.'"
   Save
28. Imagine, how glad the Queen was when she heard the name! And when soon afterwards the little man came in, and asked, "Now, Mistress Queen, what is my name?" at first she said, "Is your name Conrad?
29. "No."
30. "Is your name Harry?"
31. "No."
32. "Perhaps your name is Rumpelstiltskin?"
33. "The devil has told you that! The devil has told you that!" cried the little man, and in his anger he plunged his right foot so deep into the earth that his whole leg went in and he was stuck there forever.
   The End

Exercises

1. Why does the miller tell the king his daughter can spin straw into gold?

   A. He wants to become rich
   B. He is scared of the king
   C. He wants to impress the king
   D. He wants to go into business with the king

2. What is a lesson that Rumpelstiltskin can learn from getting caught by the miller's daughter's messenger?

   A. Don't be greedy
   B. Don't brag
   C. Help others
   D. Be nice to everyone

3. What line from the story shows that this is the lesson Rumpelstiltskin learned by getting caught by the miller's daughter's messenger?

   A. "What will you give me if I spin the straw for you this time also?
   B. ...There was quite a ridiculous little man was jumping: he hopped upon one leg, and shouted --"Today I bake, tomorrow stew, The next I'll have the young Queen's child .Ha! glad am I that no one knew That Rumpelstiltskin I am styled.'
   C. The girl knew not how to help herself, and was crying, when the door again opened, and the little man appeared, and said, "What will you give me if I spin the straw into gold for you?
   D. "If by that time you can find out my name, then you shall you keep your child."

Re-read these 2 passages from the text: "By daybreak the King was already there, and when he saw the gold he was astonished and delighted, but his heart became only more greedy."

"The King rejoiced beyond measure at the sight, but still he did not think he had enough gold. The king had the miller's daughter taken into a still larger room full of straw, and said, "You must spin this, too, in the course of this night; but if you succeed, you shall be my wife.""

4. What do you think the word astonished and the word rejoiced mean in the above passages?

   A. Angry and cried
   B. Surprised and celebrated
   C. Surprised and fainted
   D. Calm and felt sad

Re-read paragraphs 28-32.

5. What is the most likely the reason that the Queen guessed 2 names before saying the correct one?

   A. She was still confused about what his name was
   B. She wanted to make sure she was right
   C. She liked this guessing game
   D. She wanted to torment and tease Rumpelstiltskin

6. Why does the miller's daughter become the queen?

   A. She is beautiful
   B. She is the miller's daughter and that is an important title
   C. The king thinks she can turn straw into gold
   D. The king wants to go into business with the miller

Notes

Find detailed video explanations to each problem on: **ArgoPrep.com**

From Autobiography of a Monkey **The Ways of Men** By Albert Bigelow Paine

1.   I left the jungle when I thought life
2.   was hard to a far distant country
3.   On a drift that they said was a ship,
4.   And I studied the ways of my master
5.   And learned much by the trip.

6.   And we sailed to his home in fair Naples,
7.   Where I studied the language of men,
8.   And I sat on a bench with his children,
9.   But soon we went sailing again.

10.   And I made some nice friends on the voyage,
11.   And engaged in a pretty romance.
12.   I charmed all the ladies by climbing,
13.   And one of them taught me to dance.

14.   Yet often I longed for the jungle—
15.   Even its nonstop noise and the rustle of wing—
16.   And sometimes at night in my slumber
17.   I talked with our elephant king.

18.   One morning my master awoke me,
19.   And, dressed in a fancy new suit,
20.   I beheld the New World in the sunlight,
21.   And lifted my hat in salute.

22.   And then began troubles and trials—
23.   Through the streets by a string I was led;
24.   Working hard all the day for my master,
25.   Yet oft going hungry to bed.

26.   But he sold me at last to a circus
27.   And my life became easier then,
28.   So I gave many moments of free time
29.   To learning the habits of men.

30.   I copied their manners and customs
31.   I made of each fashion a note;
32.   And the children admired my performance
33.   And the ladies the cut of my coat.

34.   By and by I was sold to a banker
35.   Who was charmed with my ball-rolling feat,
36.   And dressed in a funny type costume
37.   I passed all my time on the street.

38.   But alas for my plans of the future!
39.   He died without leaving a cent,
40.   And I had to go out to hard labor
41.   To pay for my food and rent;

42.   Till I met with a gentleman's driver
43.   Who was like me in manner and face,
44.   And I told him some stories that pleased him
45.   And bribed him to give me his place.

46.   Then I started to serve my new master—
47.   A smart and fast driver was he,
48.   Who quickly saw through my trick
49.   And made an offer to me.

50.   Said he: "You're a monkey, you rascal,'
51.   And an excellent type of the brood;
52.   Let's play a good joke on the people
53.   By passing you off as a dude."

54.   So he took me at first to his barber,
55.   Who shaved me and shortened my hair,
56.   And the last single trace of the jungle
57.   Was gone when I rose from his chair.

58.   And then to his tailor and hatter—
59.   His stylist and all of the rest,
60.   Till at night I was changed from a monkey
61.   To a man most stylishly dressed.

62.   And standing alone and reflecting
63.   I thought of the why and the how,
64.   And I wondered what the snakes were doing
65.   And what would the jungle say, now.

A stanza is like a paragraph in poetry. In this poem each line is its own stanza.

Exercises

Re-read the last stanza.

1. What do you think the monkey was thinking at the end of the poem?

A. "I wish I could show them how great my life is"
B. "Through the ups and the downs I love it here!"
C. Through the ups and the downs I wish I was back in the jungle."
D. "I wish the snakes would come visit me."

Re read the 6th stanza.

2. What do you think the line, "Through the streets by a string I was led;" most likely means?

A. He was tied up on a string and led down the street
B. He was tricked by following a string
C. He followed his master without question and it wasn't good for him
D. He was tricked by his master to get into trouble and fights

Re-read lines 50 and 53.

3. What do you think the word "brood" most likely means?

A. Blood
B. Specific type of monkey
C. Group
D. Animal

4. What do you think the moral of this poem could be?

A. You should take risks and try new things
B. Don't let others boss you around
C. Do unto others as you want others to do unto you
D. Appreciate what you have and where you came from

5. An autobiography is a _____. The author of this autobiography is _____.

A. Book written by the author about the themselves; Albert Bigelow Paine writing about a pretend monkey he knows
B. Book written by the author about themselves; Albert Bigelow Paine writing pretending to be a monkey telling his life story
C. Book written about someone else's life; Albert Bigelow Paine writing about a pretend monkey he knows
D. Book written about someone else's life; Albert Bigelow Paine writing pretending to be a monkey telling his life story

Carefully re-read stanza 11.

6. Who gave the monkey his job as a driver?

A. A human driver
B. A monkey dressed as a driver
C. A human driver who looked like a monkey
D. A human who acted like a monkey

Adapted Selection from **Red Badge of Courage** *by Stephen Crane*

1. Henry had burned several times to enlist. Tales of great war-readying movements shook the land. They might not be famous, but there seemed to be much glory in them. He had read of marches, protests, conflicts, and he had longed to see it all. His busy mind had drawn for him large pictures of extravagant color, filled with righteous actions.

2. But his mother had discouraged him. She looked upon him with disapproval due of his love for the war and patriotism. She could calmly seat herself and with no difficulty give him many hundreds of reasons why he was of so much more importance on the farm than on the field of battle.

3. She had had ways of expression that told him that her statements on the subject came from the heart.

4. At last, however, the newspapers, the gossip of the village, his own imagination had excited him to a new degree. They men were fighting finely down there. Almost every day the newspapers printed stories of a decisive victory.

5. One night, as Henry lay in bed, as the winds whipped the church bells by themselves, someone pulled the rope attached to the church bell to frantically to tell the twisted news of the start of a great battle of war.

6. The noise of the people rejoicing in the night had made him shiver in a prolonged excitement. He had made up his mind.

7. Soon after, he had gone down to his mother's room and had spoken thus: "Ma, I'm going to enlist."

8. "Henry, don't you be a fool," his mother had replied. "Only boys who don't got no profession, enlist."

9. She had then covered her face with the quilt. "I'm going to join up because it's the right thing to do." Henry muttered to himself as he walked back to his room. There was an end to the matter for that night.

10. Nevertheless, the next morning he had gone to a town that was near his mother's farm and had enlisted in a company that was forming there. When he had returned home his mother was milking the brindle cow.

11. Four others stood waiting for Henry. "Ma, I've enlisted," he had said to her shyly. There was a short silence. "The Lord's will be done, Henry," she had finally replied, and had then continued to milk the brindle cow.

12. Later, when he had stood in the doorway with his soldier's clothes on his back, and with the light of excitement in his eyes helping to lessen the regret of leaving home, he had seen two tears leaving their trails on his mother's cheeks.

13. Still, she had disappointed him by saying nothing whatsoever. He had privately gotten himself ready for a beautiful scene.

14. He had prepared certain sentences, which he thought could be used with touching effect. But her words destroyed his plans. She had angrily peeled potatoes and addressed him as follows:

15. "You watch out, Henry, an' take good care of yerself in this here fighting business--you watch, an' take good care of yerself. Don't go a-thinkin' you can lick the whole rebel army at the start, because yeh can't. Yer jest one little feller amongst a whole lot of others, and yeh've got to keep quiet an' do what they tell you. I know how you will, Henry.

16. "I've knit you eight pair of socks, Henry, and I've put in all your best shirts, because I want my boy to be just as warm and comfortable as anybody in the army. Whenever they get holes in 'em, I want you to send 'em right-away back to me, so I can mend them.

 **TIP** of the **DAY**

When you see a word that you don't understand, go back and re-read the whole sentence and see if you can figure out its meaning using the words around it.

Exercises

1. What phrase helped you understand the meaning of the word enlist?

   A. "Only boys who don't got no profession, enlist."
   B. "I'm going to join up because it's the right thing to do."
   C. "The Lord's will be done, Henry,"
   D. The noise of the people rejoicing in the night had made him shiver in a prolonged excitement.

Read paragraphs 5 & 6 from the story.

3. What causes Henry to tell his mother he is enlisting?

   A. The wind whipping the church bells motivated him
   B. The sound of people rejoicing in the night inspired him
   C. The person who frantically rang the church bell scares him into enlisting
   D. The church bells reminded him of his religious duties

2. Why does Henry tell his mother "shyly" that he is going to enlist?

   A. He is scared of going to war
   B. He is a shy person
   C. He is worried what his mother might think
   D. He is scared of his mother

4. The phrase, "Don't go a-thinkin' you can lick the whole rebel army at the start, because yeh can't" shows that

   A. Henry's mother doesn't believe in his ability to feed the whole army
   B. Henry's mother doesn't think that Henry will do well at the start of the war
   C. Henry's mother is worried that Henry will be over-excited and make mistakes at the start of the war
   D. Henry's mother is worried the start of the war will be very gruesome

5. In the passage "Red Badge of Courage," Henry's mother's feelings change. How do paragraphs 11 to 15 show a change in Henry's mother's feelings? Be sure to use 2 details from the text to support your answer.

6. Summarize the story "Red Badge of Courage." Be sure to use 2 details from the text to support your answer.

WEEK 2

VIDEO
EXPLANATIONS

ARGOPREP.COM

The Lad Who Went to the North Wind

1. Once upon a time there was an old widow who had one son and, as she was poorly and weak, her son had to go up into the safe to fetch meal for cooking; but when he got outside the safe, and was just going down the steps, there came the North Wind, puffing and blowing, the North Wind caught up the meal, and went away with it through the air. Then the lad went back into the safe for more; but when he came out again on the steps, the North Wind took the meal with a puff; and more than that, he did so the third time. At this the lad got very angry; and thought to himself that the North Wind should behave so. He had an idea, he thought he'd just look him up, and ask him to give up his meal.

2. So off he went, but the way was long, and he walked and walked; but at last he came to the North Wind's house.

3. "Good day!" said the lad, and "thank you for coming to see us yesterday."

4. "GOOD DAY!" answered the North Wind, for his voice was loud and gruff, "AND THANKS FOR COMING TO SEE ME. WHAT DO YOU WANT?"

5. "Oh!" answered the lad, "I only wished to ask you to be so good as to let me have back that meal you took from me on the safe steps, for we haven't much to live on; and if you're to go on snapping up the morsel we have there'll be nothing for us but to starve."

6. "I haven't got your meal," said the North Wind; "but if you are in such need, I'll give you a cloth which will get you everything you want, if you only say, 'Cloth, spread yourself, and serve up all kinds of good dishes!'"

7. With this the lad was satisfied. But, as the way home was so long he couldn't get home in one day, he stopped in an inn on the way; and when they were going to sit down to supper, he laid the cloth on a table which stood in the corner and said:

8. "Cloth spread yourself, and serve up all kinds of good dishes."

9. He had not said so before, but the cloth did as it was told; and all who stood by thought it was an amazing thing, but most of all the landlady. So, when all were fast asleep, at dead of night, she took the lad's cloth, and put another in its place, just like the one he had got from the North Wind, but one which couldn't so much as serve up so much as a bit of dry bread.

10. So, when the lad woke, he took his cloth and went off with it, and that day he got home to his mother.

11. "Now," said he, "I've been to the North Wind's house, and a good fellow he is, for he gave me this cloth, and when I only say to it, 'Cloth, spread yourself, and serve up all kinds of good dishes,' I get any sort of food I please."

12. "All very true, I dare say," said his mother; "but seeing is believing, and I shan't believe it till I see it."

13. So the lad quickly drew out a table, laid the cloth on it, and said:

14. "Cloth, spread yourself, and serve all up kinds of good dishes."

15. But not a bit of dry bread did the cloth serve up.

16. "Well," said the lad, "there's nothing we can do but to go to the North Wind again;" and away he went.

17. So he came to where the North Wind lived late in the afternoon.

18. "Good evening!" said the lad.

19. "Good evening," said the North Wind.

When reading fiction stories think about each character as a whole. Go back to all of their actions and think to yourself, "what does this tell me about this character?"

20. "I want my rights for that meal of ours which you took," said the lad; "as for that cloth I got, it isn't worth a penny."
21. "I've got no meal," said the North Wind; "but you can have a ram which makes nothing but golden coins as soon as you say to it:
22. "'Ram, ram! make money!'"
23. So the lad thought this an amazing thing, but as it was too far to get home that day, he turned in for the night to the same inn where he had slept before.
24. Before he did anything, he tried what the North Wind had said of the ram, and found it to be true; but when the landlord saw that, she thought it was a famous ram, and, when the lad had fallen asleep, she took another ram which, couldn't coin gold and changed the two.
25. Next morning off went the lad; and when he got home to his mother he said:
26. "After all, the North Wind is a jolly fellow; for now he has given me a ram which can coin gold if I only say, 'Ram, ram! make money!'"
27. "All very true, I dare say," said his mother; "but I shan't believe any such stuff until I see the gold made."
28. "Ram, ram! make money!" said the lad; but if the ram made anything it wasn't money.
29. So the lad went back again to the North Wind and let him have it, he said the ram was worth nothing, and he must have his rights for the meal.
30. "Well," said the North Wind; "I've nothing else to give you but that old stick in the corner over there; but it's a stick of that kind that if you say:
31. "'Stick, stick! Fight on!' it fights on till you say:
32. "'Stick, stick! now stop!'"
33. So, as the way was long, the lad turned in this night too to the landlord; but as he could pretty well guess how things would turn out as to the cloth and the ram, he lay down at once on the bench and began to snore, as if he were asleep.
34. Now the landlord, who easily excited saw that the stick thought it must be worth something. She hunted up one which was like it, and when she heard the lad snore, she was going to change the two, but just as the landlord was about to take it the lad bawled out:
35. "Stick, stick! Fight on!"
36. So the stick began to beat the landlord, till she jumped over chairs, and tables, and benches, and yelled and roared:
37. "Oh my! oh my! tell the stick be still, or else it will beat me to death, and you shall have back both your cloth and your ram."
38. When the lad thought the landlord had got enough, he said:
39. "Stick, stick! now stop!"
40. Then he took the cloth and put it into his pocket, and went home with his stick in his hand, leading the ram by a leash round its horns; and so he got his rights for the meal he had lost.
The End

Exercises

1. What 2 words best characterize the North Wind in this story?

   A. Greedy and mean
   B. Selfish but thoughtful
   C. Generous and kind
   D. Sad and hard working

2. Which statement shows the North Wind and the lad's relationship?

   A. North Wind was helpful to the lad because he liked helping others
   B. North Wind was helpful to the lad because he had stolen his food in the beginning
   C. The lad liked helping the North Wind because he was powerful
   D. The lad liked helping the North Wind get his food back

3. Which best describes the moral (theme) of the story?

   A. Don't talk to strangers
   B. Two wrongs don't make a right
   C. Being greedy never works out
   D. If you make a mistake just keep going

4. Which phrase best shows the moral (theme) of the story?

   A. "Oh my! oh my! bid the stick be still, or else it will beat me to death, and you shall have back both your cloth and your ram."
   B. I haven't got your meal," said the North Wind; "but if you are in such need, I'll give you a cloth which will get you everything you want.
   C. After all, the North Wind is a jolly fellow; for now he has given me a ram which can coin gold if I only say, 'Ram, ram! make money!'"
   D. "All very true, I dare say," said his mother; "but seeing is believing, and I shan't believe it till I see it."

5. What is most likely the reason the North Wind keeps giving the young lad magical things?

   A. He likes the young lad
   B. He likes giving things to charity
   C. He is sad that he is poor
   D. He feels bad for taking the lad's food in the beginning

Re-read paragraph 5.

6. What do you think the word morsel means in this sentence?

   A. Food
   B. Little bits
   C. Lots of food
   D. Bird

Notes

Eli Whitney and the Cotton Gin

1. The cotton industry is one of the most ancient. One or more of the many species of the cotton plant is local to four continents: Asia, Africa, and the Americas, and the manufacture of the fiber into yarn and cloth seems to have developed independently in each of them. We find mention of cotton in India fifteen hundred years before Christ.

2. Alexander the Great introduced cotton into Europe. The East India Company imported cotton fabrics into England early in the seventeenth century, and these fabrics made their way in spite of the bitter fight put up by the people with wool interests, which were at times strong enough to have the use of cotton cloth prohibited by law.

3. In the New World, the Spanish explorers found cotton and cotton fabrics in use everywhere. Columbus, Cortes, Pizarro, Magellan, and others speak of the various uses to which the fiber was put, and admired what the natives made from cotton. It seems probable that cotton was in use in the New World quite as early as in India.

4. The first English settlers in America found little or no cotton among the natives. But they soon began to import the fiber from the West Indies, and when the plant itself came into contact with the warm soil and climate of the Southern colonies the crop grew easily. During the colonial period, however, cotton never became the leading crop; it was hardly an important crop. Cotton could be grown profitably only where there was a large supply of exceedingly cheap labor, and labor in America, white or black, was never and could never be as cheap as in India. American slaves could be much more usefully employed in the farming of rice and indigo.

5. Three varieties of the cotton plant were grown in the South. Two kinds of the black-seed or long-staple variety thrived in the sea-islands and along the coast from Delaware to Georgia, but only the hardier and more important green-seed or short-staple cotton could be raised inland.

6. The labor of farming and harvesting cotton of any kind was very great. The fiber, growing in bolls like a walnut in size and shape, had to be taken by hand from every boll, for no satisfactory cotton harvester has yet been invented.

7. But in the case of the green-seed or upland cotton, the only kind which could ever be grown extensively in the South, there was another and more serious problem in the way, namely, the difficulty of separating the fiber from the seeds. No machine yet devised could perform this tedious and unprofitable task.

8. The quickest and most skillful pair of hands could separate only a pound or two of lint from its three pounds of seeds in an ordinary working day. Usually the task was taken up at the end of the day, when the other work was done. It was also the regular task for a rainy day. It is not surprising, that cotton was not used often. In 1783 wool made up about seventy-seven percent, flax about eighteen percent, and cotton only about five per cent of the clothing of the people of Europe and the United States.

9. The romance of cotton begins on a New England farm. It was on a farm in the town (township) of Westboro, in Worcester County, Massachusetts, in the year 1765, that Eli Whitney, inventor of the cotton gin, was born. We are told that young Eli displayed a passion for tools almost as soon as he could walk, that he made a violin at the age of twelve and about the same time took his father's watch to pieces sneakily and succeeded in putting it together again so successfully to avoid his father ever finding out.

TIP of the DAY

Non-fiction stories usually contain lots of information. Some of it isn't important and some of it will be asked about in the questions. Make sure to preview the questions to know what you should be looking for.

10. Like so many young New Englanders of the time, Whitney sought employment in the South. His partner, Phineas Miller, was a cultivated New England gentleman, a graduate of Yale College, who, like Whitney, had sought his fortune as a teacher in the South.

11. At the outset the partners failed seriously in their plan for commercializing the invention. But they eventually succeeded at the creation of the cotton gin, which easily separates the cottonseeds from their fibers.

12. Other important results followed on the invention of the cotton gin. In 1793 slavery seemed a dying tradition, North and South. Conditions of soil and climate made slavery unsuccessful in the North. On many of the indigo, rice, and tobacco plantations in the South there were more slaves than could be helpfully employed, and many planters were thinking of emancipating their slaves, when along came this simple but wonderful machine and with it the vision of great riches in cotton.

13. For a while slaves could not earn their keep separating the cotton from its seeds by hand, but they could earn enormous profits in the fields, once the difficulty of extracting the seeds was solved. Slaves were no longer a problem but an advantage. The price of "field hands" rose, and continued to rise. Cotton became King of the South.

14. The supposed economic need of slave labor led great men to defend slavery, and politics in the South became largely the defense of slavery against the free North. The fight between the North and the South became more and more aggressive. Then came the Civil War.

Exercises

1. Who do you think the author was talking about when he said "people with wool interests?"

  A. People who love sheep
  B. People who make a living out of selling wool
  C. People who like the way wool feels compared to cotton
  D. People who are interested in how to make wool

4. Which is the best at describing the meaning of the word "profitable?"

  A. Cheap
  B. Easy
  C. Hard
  D. Money making

Re-read paragraph 4.

2. Which statement best describes how people living in the New World felt about cotton?

  A. There was a lot of cotton available due to trade and people loved using it
  B. There was a lot of cotton because it grew easily and people loved using it
  C. There was a lot of cotton because it grew easily but people didn't use it much at first
  D. There wasn't a lot of cotton and people wanted more

5. Which statement is true about life before Eli Whitney invented the cotton gin?

  A. People loved cotton and needed a cheaper faster way to get to it
  B. People didn't use cotton often because separating the seeds from the cotton fiber was hard and expensive
  C. People were sick of wool so this invention sparked the cotton revolution
  D. The end of slavery created a need for an invention that separated the cotton fiber from the seed quickly

3. Why was the cotton gin an important invention?

  A. It made it easier and faster to separate the cotton fiber from the seeds
  B. It made it easier to turn the cotton into cloth
  C. Slave owners were happy that slaves didn't have to work so hard anymore
  D. It was the first invention to use electricity

6. Which statement best describes an effect of the invention of the cotton gin?

  A. Slavery ended shortly after the invention of the cotton gin
  B. The cost of slave labor decreased because the work was easier now
  C. The cost of slave labor went back up because there was more work to be done
  D. Slaves were happier because the work was easier

Notes

 ARGOPREP

Find detailed video explanations to each problem on:
ArgoPrep.com

The Glory of Gettysburg

THE BATTLE

1. The Civil War, fought from 1861-1865 matched the North states calling themselves the Union against the southern states calling themselves the Confederacy against one another locked in a war fought largely over whether slavery should be allowed.

2. The Battle of Gettysburg, which raged through July 1st, 2nd and 3rd, in 1863, was called the "high water mark" of the Civil War, and one of the "fifteen most important battles" of history. It was important because General Robert E. Lee, the lead general for the confederates (the south), with his brave army, was driven back from Gettysburg, Pennsylvania. If Lee had won there, he might have destroyed Philadelphia and New York. Then he could have surrounded and captured Baltimore and Washington. This would have changed the grand result of the war.

3. In numbers, bravery and genius, the battle of Gettysburg was the greatest that had ever been fought up to that time.

4. It came at a terrible time in the war, when everything seemed to be going against the Union (the north). There had been four terrible defeats—twice at Bull Run, followed by Fredericksburg and Chancellorsville. General Lee had made his way north into Pennsylvania for a battle at Gettysburg, but victory there was anything but certain.

5. The union had actually won the battle! But, after winning the battle of Gettysburg, which the President (Abraham Lincoln) hoped would end the war, the new leader of the Union army, General Meade made an announcement. He announced that he had defeated the Confederate army, and stated that he had "driven the invaders from our soil." Mr. Lincoln fell on his knees and, covering his face with his great, strong hands, cried out in tears of agony:

6. "'Driven the invaders from our soil.' My God, is that all?"

7. But Lincoln's spirits were bound to rise. Believing he was "on God's side," he felt that the cause of right could not lose. Keeping the country together and ending slavery were righteous causes.

8. The next day, July 4th, 1863, came the surrender of Vicksburg, the stronghold of the great West held by the Confederates. Joy began to cover his thin and pale skin, and the light of hope shone again in his deep, gray eyes.

THE ADDRESS

9. Not long after the conflict at Gettysburg a movement was started to dedicate a large part of that battleground to a national cemetery.

10. The Hon. Edward Everett, an expert in national and educational matters, and the greatest living spokesman, was invited to deliver the grand speech. The President was asked if he could, to come and make a few remarks, but Mr. Everett was to be the main speaker of the occasion.

11. The Sunday before the date of the dedication, the President went with his friend to a garden where he had promised to sit for a photograph. While there he showed his friend a copy of Everett's speech, which had been sent to him. As this speech covered two newspaper pages, Mr. Lincoln struck an attitude and quoted from a speech by Daniel Webster:

This passage has short response questions that will ask you to use details from the text. Save time by underlining those details as you read.

12. "Solid men of Boston, make no long speeches!" and burst out laughing. When Mr. Brooks asked about his speech for that occasion, Mr. Lincoln replied: "I've got it written, but not licked into shape yet. It's short, short, short!"

13. About noon on the 19th of November, the presidential party arrived in a parade and took seats on the stage made for the ceremony. The President was seated in a rocking chair placed there for him. There were fifteen thousand people waiting, some of whom had been standing in the sun for hours

14. A youth who stood near the stage in front of the President says that, while Mr. Everett was talking, Mr. Lincoln took his "little speech," as he called it, out of his pocket, and looked it over like a schoolboy with a half-learned lesson. The President had put the finishing touches on it that morning. As it was likely that the President would make a few offhand remarks, no one seems to have noticed its simple greatness until it was printed in the newspapers.

15. Yet Mr. Lincoln was interrupted four or five times during the two minutes by applause. The fact that the President was speaking was enough, no matter what he said. The people would have applauded Abraham Lincoln if he had merely listed the multiplication table! When he finished, they gave "three times three cheers" for the President of the United States, and three cheers for each of the State Governors present.

Exercises

1. Which statement best helps you understand the phrase "high water mark," in paragraph 2?

   A. One of the "fifteen most important battles" of history
   B. It was important because General Robert E. Lee, the lead general for the confederates (the south), with his brave army, was driven back from Gettysburg, Pennsylvania
   C. This would have changed the grand result of the war.
   D. In numbers and bravery and genius, the battle of Gettysburg was the greatest that had ever been fought up to that time

Re-read paragraphs 5 & 6.

2. Which statement shows how Abraham Lincoln felt about the victory at Gettysburg?

   A. The union was winning the war before the battle at Gettysburg, so Lincoln was upset when they didn't do more than just "'Drive the invaders from our soil!"
   B. The union was losing the war before the battle at Gettysburg, so Lincoln was upset when they didn't do more than just "'Drive the invaders from our soil!"
   C. Lincoln was happy that the Union had won the battle at Gettysburg.
   D. Lincoln was happy that they were winning the war and Gettysburg was just another battle

Exercises

3. What is the difference between Edward Everett's speech and Abraham Lincoln's speech?

A. Everett wrote a better speech the Lincoln

B. Everett didn't plan his speech and Lincoln did

C. Lincoln wrote a longer speech

D. Lincoln planned only a little of his short speech but Everett wrote a long and planned out speech

4. Why was the battle of Gettysburg important?

A. Because a great speech came after

B. Because if the Union would have lost this battle General Lee might have taken over other cities and towns as well

C. Because the Union captured the Confederate soldiers

D. Because it won the war for the Union

5. The union forces won the battle of Gettysburg. Why was this victory important? Give 2 examples from the text to support your answer.

_____

_____

_____

_____

_____

6. The Gettysburg Address given by President Abraham Lincoln is one of the most famous speeches in history. The way he prepared and what he wrote was different from Everett's speech. How was it different? Give 2 examples from the passage about how his preparation for the speech or the actual speech was different from Everett's.

_____

_____

_____

_____

_____

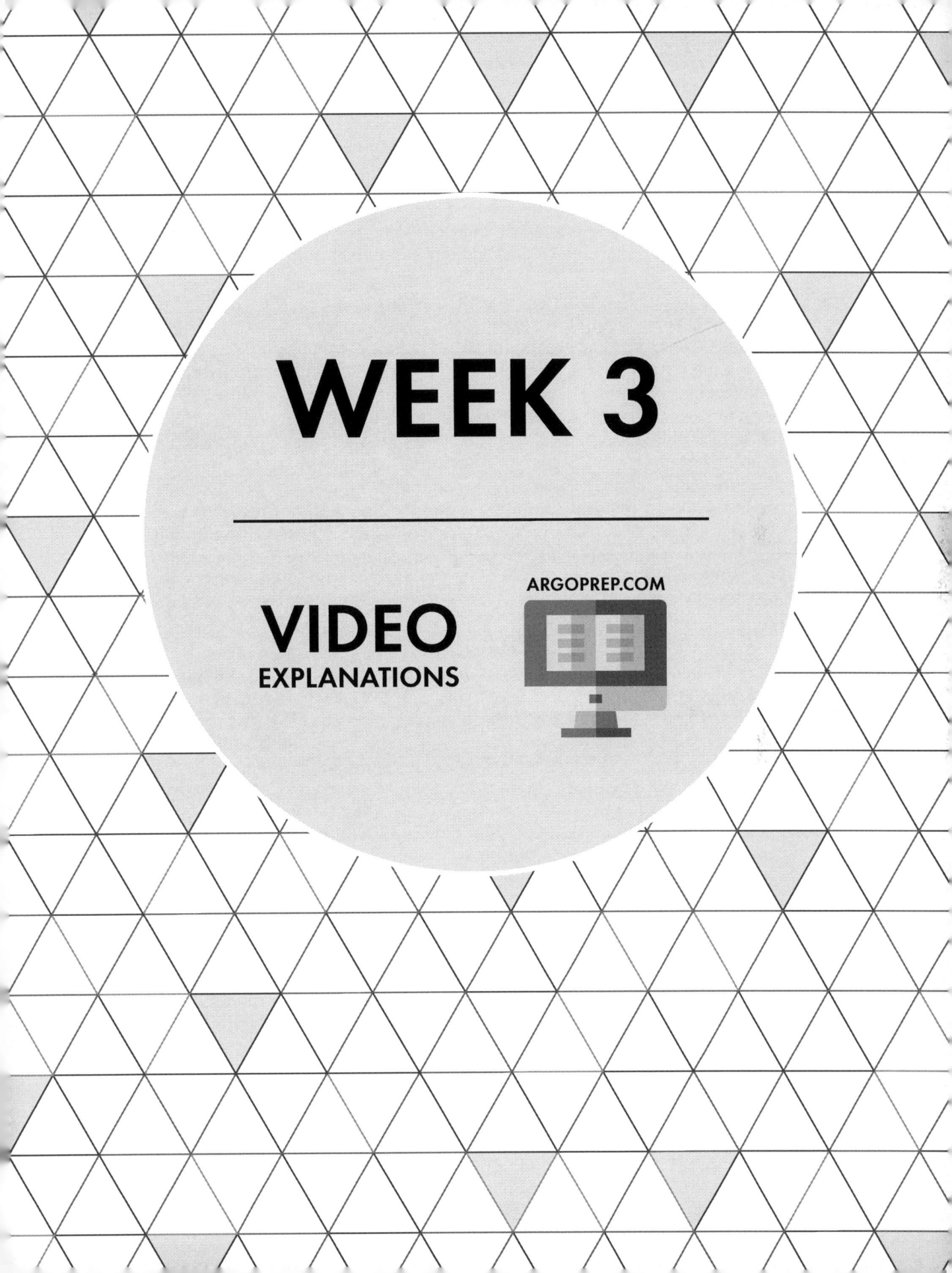

WEEK 3

VIDEO
EXPLANATIONS

ARGOPREP.COM

How the Camel got his Hump

1. In the beginning of years, when the world was so new and all, and the Animals were just beginning to work for Man, there was a Camel, and he lived in the middle of a Howling Desert because he did not want to work; and besides, he was a Howler himself. So he ate sticks and thorns and milkweed and prickles, and was most lazy; and when anybody spoke to him he said 'Humph!' Just 'Humph!' and no more.

2. The Horse came to him on Monday morning, with a saddle on his back and a bit in his mouth, and said, 'Camel, O Camel, come out and trot like the rest of us.'

3. 'Humph!' said the Camel; and the Horse went away and told the Man.

4. Next, the Dog came to him, with a stick in his mouth, and said, 'Camel, O Camel, come and fetch and carry like the rest of us.'

5. 'Humph!' said the Camel; and the Dog went away and told the Man.

6. Finally the Ox came to him, with the load on his neck and said, 'Camel, O Camel, come and work like the rest of us.'

7. 'Humph!' said the Camel; and the Ox went away and told the Man.

8. At the end of the day the Man called the Horse and the Dog and the Ox together, and said, 'Three, O Three, I'm very sorry for you (with the world so new-and-all); but that Humph-thing in the Desert can't work, or he would have been here by now, so I am going to leave him alone, and you must work double-time to make up for it.'

9. That made the Three very angry (with the world so new-and-all), and they held a fuss, a protest and a pow-wow on the edge of the Desert; and the Camel came chewing milkweed most lazily, and laughed at them. Then he said 'Humph!' and went away again.

10. Then there came along the Djinn in charge of All Deserts, rolling in a cloud of dust (Djinns always travel that way because it is Magic), and he stopped to discuss and pow-pow with the Three.

11. 'Djinn of All Deserts,' said the Horse, 'is it right for anyone to be idle, with the world so new-and-all?'

12. 'Certainly not,' said the Djinn.

13. 'Well,' said the Horse, 'there's a thing in the middle of your Howling Desert (and he's a Howler himself) with a long neck and long legs, and he hasn't done a stroke of work since Monday morning. He won't trot.'

14. 'Whew!' said the Djinn, whistling, 'that's my Camel, What does he say about it?'

15. 'He says "Humph!"' said the Dog; 'and he won't fetch and carry.'

16. 'Does he say anything else?'

17. 'Only "Humph; and he won't work,' said the Ox.

18. 'Very good,' said the Djinn. 'I'll deal with him if you will kindly wait a minute.'

19. The Djinn rolled himself up in his dust-cloud, and took off across the desert, and found the Camel most lazily, looking at his own reflection in a pool of water.

20. 'My long and bubbly friend,' said the Djinn, 'what's this I hear of your doing no work, with the world so new-and-all?'

21. 'Humph!' said the Camel.

 *Sometimes even passages that contain only multiple choice questions will be linked. When reading the next 2 passages be sure to think about them together.*

22. The Djinn sat down, with his chin in his hand, and began to think a Great Magic, while the Camel looked at his own reflection in the pool of water.

23. 'You've given the Three extra work ever since Monday morning, all on account of your laziness,' said the Djinn; and he went on thinking of magic, with his chin in his hand.

24. 'Humph!' said the Camel.

25. 'I shouldn't say that again if I were you,' said the Djinn; 'you might say it once too often. Camel, I want you to work.'

26. And the Camel said 'Humph!' again; but no sooner had he said it than he saw his back, that he was so proud of, puffing up and puffing up into a great big lolloping humph.

27. 'Do you see that?' said the Djinn. 'That's your very own humph that you've brought upon your very own self by not working. Today is Thursday, and you've done no work since Monday, when the work began. Now you are going to work.'

28. 'How can I,' said the Camel, 'with this humph on my back?'

29. 'That's made a-purpose,' said the Djinn, 'all because you missed those three days. You will be able to work now for three days without eating, because you can live on your humph; and don't you ever say I never did anything for you. Come out of the Desert and go to the Three, and behave.'

30. And the Camel worked, humph and all, and went away to join the Three. And from that day to this the Camel always wears a humph (we call it 'hump' now, not to hurt his feelings); but he has never yet caught up with the three days that he missed at the beginning of the world, and he has never yet learned how to behave.

Exercises

1. What happened when the Camel didn't work?

    A. The Horse, Dog and Ox also did no work in protest
    B. They punished the Camel
    C. The Horse, Dog and Ox had to do extra work
    D. The Horse, Dog and Ox punished the Camel

Re - read paragraph 11.

2. What do you think the world idle most likely means?

    A. Happy
    B. Hard - working
    C. Lazy
    D. Funny

3. Which statement best describes the Djinn's role in the story?

    A. The leader of the desert with magic powers
    B. Another animal with magic powers
    C. A man who listens to the animals' problems from the start
    D. A wise man who gives advice

4. Why did the Djinn give the camel a hump at the end of the story?

    A. To teach him a lesson not to say humph anymore
    B. To teach him a lesson that if you're lazy you'll get a hump on your back
    C. The hump stores food and water so the camel can work for days without stopping
    D. The Djinn punished the camel by adding a funny looking hump on his back

5. Which of the following is a solution that the Three try to get the camel to help?

    A. They went the Djinn for help
    B. They showed the camel how easy the work was
    C. They complained to the man they were working for
    D. They got all the other animals together to protest

6. Why doesn't the man make the camel help the Three?

    A. He doesn't want any trouble with the camel
    B. He knows the Three can do the work even better
    C. He knows the camel is lazy and won't help
    D. He likes the camel and doesn't want to make him work.

Notes

Camel's Hump

1.   The Camel's hump is an ugly lump
2.   Which well you may see at the Zoo;
3.   But uglier yet is the hump we get
4.   From having too little to do.

5.   Kiddies and grown-ups too-oo-oo,
6.   If we haven't enough to do-oo-oo,
7.   We get the hump—
8.   Cameelious hump—
9.   The hump that is black and blue!

10. We climb out of bed with a cranky head
11. And a snarly-yarly voice.
12. We shiver and scowl and we grunt and we growl
13. At our bath and our boots and our toys;

14. And there ought to be a corner for me
15. (And I know there is one for you)
16. When we get the hump—
17. Cameelious hump—

18. The hump that is black and blue!
19. The cure for this ill is not to sit still,
20. Or frown with a book by the fire;
21. But to take a large hoe and a shovel also,
22. And dig till you gently perspire (sweat);

23. And then you will find that the sun and the wind,
24. And the Djinn of the Garden too,
25. Have lifted the hump—
26. The horrible hump—
27. The hump that is black and blue!

28. I get it as well as you-oo-oo—
29. If I haven't enough to do-oo-oo—
30. We all get hump—
31. Cameelious hump—
32. Kiddies and grown-ups too!

TIP of the DAY

Poems sometimes contain nonsense words. If you can understand the meaning of the line and or poem, move on!

Exercises

1. What is most likely the theme of this poem?

   A. Follow the rules and you won't get a hump
   B. There can be consequences for being lazy and not doing your best work
   C. Camels can't be trusted
   D. Kids and grown ups should respect each other

2. What is the relationship between stanza 3 and stanza 4?

   A. Stanza 3 shows what happens if you have a hump and stanza 4 shows how not to get the hump
   B. Stanza 3 shows how not to get the hump and stanza 4 shows what happens if you have a hump
   C. Stanza 3 shows the cause of getting a hump and stanza 4 shows the effect of getting a hump
   D. Stanza 3 and stanza 4 aren't related

3. How can you avoid getting a hump?

   A. Stay far away from the Djinn
   B. Make sure you're nice to all your friends
   C. Be lazy
   D. Work hard

4. Which stanza shows how to avoid getting a hump?

   A. Stanza 1
   B. Stanza 7
   C. Stanza 6
   D. Stanza 5

5. How is the poem and story about the camel related?

   A. The story shows how the camel got his hump and the poem does too
   B. The story shows how the camel got his hump and the poem shows the reader how to avoid getting a hump
   C. The poem and the story are not related
   D. The poem shows how the camel got his hump and the story shows how you can avoid getting a hump

6. What do you think the author's purpose was for writing this poem?

   A. To inform
   B. To entertain
   C. To persuade
   D. To teach us how not to get a hump

 Find detailed video explanations to each problem on:
ArgoPrep.com

Aladdin, and the Wonderful Lamp

1. Aladdin was the son of a poor tailor in an Eastern city. He was a spoiled boy, and loved play better than work; so that when Mustapha, his father, died, he was not able to earn his living; and his poor mother had to spin cotton all day long to get food. But she dearly loved her son, knowing that he had a good heart, and she believed that as he grew older he would do better, and become at last a worthy and well-off man.

2. One day, when Aladdin was walking outside the town, an old man came up to him, and looking very hard in his face, said he was his father's brother, and had long been away in a distant country, but that now he wished to help his nephew to get on. He then put a ring on the boy's finger, telling him that no harm could happen to him so long as he wore it. Now, this strange man was no uncle of Aladdin, nor was he related at all to him; but he was a wicked magician, who wanted to make use of the lad's services, as we shall see presently.

3. The old man led Aladdin a good way into the country, until they came to a very lonely spot between two lofty black mountains. Here he lighted a fire, and threw into it some gum, all the time repeating many strange words. The ground then opened just before them, and a stone trap-door appeared.

4. After lifting this up, the Magician told Aladdin to go below, down some broken steps, and at the foot of these he would find three halls, in the last of which was a door leading to a garden full of beautiful trees; this he was to cross, and after some more steps, he would come to a porch, on which there was a lighted Lamp. He was then to take the Lamp, put out the light, empty the oil, and bring it away with him.

5. Aladdin found all the Magician had told him to be true; he passed quickly but cautiously through the three halls, so as not even to touch the walls with his clothes, as the Magician had directed. He took the Lamp from the porch, threw out the oil, and put it near his heart. As he came back through the garden, his eyes were dazzled with the bright-colored fruits on the trees, shining like glass.

6. Many of these he plucked and put in his pockets, and then returned with the Lamp, and called upon his uncle to help him up the broken steps. "Give me the Lamp," said the old man, angrily. "Not till I get out safe," cried the boy. The Magician, in a passion, then slammed down the trap door, and Aladdin was shut up fast enough. While crying bitterly, he by chance rubbed the ring, and a figure appeared before him, saying, "I am your slave, the Genius of the Ring; what do you desire?"

7. Aladdin told the Genius of the Ring that he only wanted to be set free, and to be taken back to his mother. In an instant he found himself at home, very hungry, and his poor mother was much pleased to see him again. He told her all that had happened; she then felt curious to look at the Lamp he had brought, and began rubbing it, to make it shine brighter.

8. Both were quite amazed when before them a strange figure appeared; this proved to be the Genius of the Lamp, who asked for their commands. On hearing that food was what they most wanted, a woman instantly entered with the choicest fare upon a dainty dish of silver, and with silver plates for them to eat from.

9. Aladdin and his mother feasted upon the rich fare brought to them, and sold the silver dish and plates, they lived happily for some weeks. Aladdin was now able to dress well, and in taking his usual walk, he one day chanced to see the Sultan's daughter.

10. He was so much struck with her beauty, that he fell in love with her at once, and told his mother that she must go to the Sultan, and ask him to give the Princess to be his wife.

  *If a question (like number 2) refers to a paragraph go back and re-read that paragraph. Use evidence only from that paragraph to help you reach your answer.*

11. The Sultan, who was amazed at their richness, and said to Aladdin's mother: "Your son shall have his wish, if he can send me, in a week, forty bowls like this, carried by twenty white and twenty black slaves, handsomely dressed." He thought of this to keep what he had gotten from Aladdin already and to hear no more of Aladdin. But the Genius of the Lamp soon brought the bowls of jewels and the slaves, and Aladdin's mother went with them to the Sultan.

12. The Sultan was overjoyed at receiving these rich gifts, and at once agreed that the Princess should be the wife of Aladdin.

13. As soon as they were married, Aladdin ordered the Genius of the Lamp to build, in the course of a night, a most superb Palace, and there the young couple lived quite happily for some time.

14. One day, when Aladdin was out hunting with the Sultan. The wicked Magician, who had heard of Aladdin's good luck wished to get hold of the Magic Lamp. He cried out in the streets, "New lamps for old ones!"

15. The princess was in the Palace, and heard the magician's cry. She traded Aladdin's magic lamp for a new one with the magician.

16. As soon as the Magician had safely got the Lamp, he caused the Genius to remove the Palace, and the princess within it, to Africa. Aladdin's grief was very great, and so was the rage of the Sultan at the loss of the Princess, and poor Aladdin's life was in some danger, for the Sultan threatened to kill him if he did not restore his daughter in three days.

17. Aladdin first called upon the Genius of the Ring to help him, but all he could do was to take him to Africa. The Princess was rejoiced to see him again, but was very sorry to find that she had been the cause of all their trouble by parting with the wonderful Lamp. Aladdin, however, comforted her, and told her that he had thought of a plan for getting it back.

18. He then left her, but soon returned with a powerful sleeping-medicine and advised her to have the Magician visit her and treat him with pretended kindness, and pour the sleeping medicine into his wine at dinner that day, so as to make him fall sound asleep, when they could take the Lamp from him. Everything happened as they expected; the Magician drank the wine, and when Aladdin came in, he found that the magician had fallen back lifeless on the couch. Aladdin took the Lamp from his grip, and called upon the Genius to transport the Palace, the Princess, and himself, back to their city.

19. Aladdin, with his princess, lived long afterwards to enjoy his good fortune.

Exercises

1. How did the Magician get the lamp from Aladdin?

  A. He slammed the trap door shut
  B. He tricked him by using magic
  C. He tricked the princess into trading Aladdin's lamp for a new one
  D. He stole it

2. How did Aladdin get the lamp back from the Magician?

  A. He stole it
  B. The princess tricked him and took it while he was sleeping
  C. Aladdin used magic to get it back
  D. He made the Sultan give it back to him

Exercises

3. How did Aladdin get the lamp to begin with?

   A. He wished for it on the magic ring
   B. He found it on his own in the desert
   C. The old man opened a hole in the ground and Aladdin had to find it inside a trap door
   D. He had it all along and it became magical

4. Why does the Sultan tell Aladdin to bring him many gifts in order to marry his daughter?

   A. So that the Sultan could be rich
   B. So the princess could have a rich husband
   C. So that Aladdin could prove he was a hard worker
   D. He thought it was impossible and he didn't want Aladdin to marry his daughter

5. In the story Aladdin and the Wonderful Lamp the Magician wants the lamp. How does he get the lamp? Use 2 examples from the text that show how he got the lamp.

6. In the story Aladdin and the Wonderful Lamp the Magician loses the lamp. How did he lose it? Use 2 examples from the text that show how the Magician lost the lamp.

WEEK 4

VIDEO
EXPLANATIONS

ARGOPREP.COM

The Law of the Jungle

1.   Hush! Here come all the animals! The buffaloes, the blue deer, the red deer, the wild pigs, the hyenas, the wolves, the red dogs, and many others. Watch and see how each kind of animal comes; it is not always in the same way. The moon is now shining clear above the trees, and we can see a long way up the stream.

2.   See the buffaloes! They come a little above the elephants. But they do not come one behind another in a line, like the elephants. They come three or four together. They also have beaten down the bushes there years ago; to make a drinking place; and it is wide enough for three or four of them to drink at the same time, side by side.

How Buffaloes Come to Drink—in Rows

3.   But why must they drink three or four at the same time? Because the buffaloes are like a body of soldiers, one row behind another. Sometimes twenty or thirty rows make up a herd. We see only the first row drinking now, but soon we shall see the others behind.

4.   And why do the buffaloes come like a body of soldiers? Because they are afraid of their enemy—the tiger! Once upon a time the buffaloes lived scattered about, and many of them got eaten by the tiger, one at a time. Then those that escaped from the tiger became wise; they joined together like a body of soldiers, so that they could beat off the tiger.

5.   But now let us watch the first row drinking. They are all bull buffaloes, the Papas of the herd; you can tell that by their huge horns, a yard long on each side of the head. You see how the buffaloes stand side by side, so that their horns almost touch one another. That is the way the buffaloes have marched to the stream from their feeding place—horn to horn. Why? Because no prowling tiger can get past those horns.

6.   Watch the first row as it finishes drinking; the whole row wheels around to the side like soldiers. Then the buffaloes that have had their drink march to the back of the herd, and stand there in a row facing the jungle.

7.   Meanwhile the second row in the front has stepped to the water to drink. These also are bull buffaloes. When they finish drinking, they also wheel, march to the back of the herd, and there stand behind the first row. In this way four or five rows of bulls drink, one after the other, and go to the back of the herd.

8.   Next come about a dozen rows of cow buffaloes and their calves, or children. You see again, like the elephants, the Mammas and children among the buffaloes are also in the middle, safe from all harm.

9.   Then at the end there are four or five rows of bull buffaloes again, to guard the Mammas and the children from enemies in the back.

Buffalo Knights Guard the Timid Deer

10. But wait a moment! Before the buffaloes go away, a most wonderful thing happens. You have read stories, how once upon a time there were brave knights who used to come to the help of ladies who were in danger. Well, you will be glad to know that these bull buffaloes are just like those brave knights. Do you see that timid little shadow creeping in by the side of the buffaloes?

 TIP of the DAY

Preview the questions. After reading the story cover the answer choices and see if you can get the answer correct on your own.

11. She is a blue deer, a very timid lady indeed; for she knows that a tiger is waiting in the high ground behind, to catch her. It is the last chance of the tiger to get his supper; so he waits by the high ground behind, and watches for some weak animal like the deer to come to drink.

12. But the blue deer knows that; so she hides in the bushes, and waits for the buffaloes to come to drink. Then as the buffaloes come to the water, row after row, horn to horn, she tries to creep in toward them; she even tries to creep in under the horns of the buffaloes, knowing that there she will be quite safe from the tiger. It takes her a long time to reach the buffaloes in that way, without being caught by the tiger.

13. The buffaloes wait a little for her! They take a little longer to drink, to give her a chance to reach the water by their side. Like the brave knights, they feel proud of helping a lady.

14. Now see! The blue deer also has finished drinking. She goes away with the buffaloes, under their horns. They all reach the jungle again. She looks carefully: the tiger is watching her, but he dares not come too near. She sees where he is—then suddenly she gives a leap—another leap—and another— quickly! The tiger leaps after her—but she leaped first! She is gone! She is safe!

The Buffaloes and the Blue Deer

15. The tiger is furious. He stands a moment before the buffaloes, growling with rage. But the bulls in front of the herd paw the ground, and rattle their horns with one another. They are going to charge!

16. But that tiger does not wait for the charge of the bull buffaloes. He does not want to be trampled into a mess under their hoofs, or cut up into pieces with their horns. Instead, he sneaks away, growling. He sneaks back to the stream, to wait for some other weak animal.

Exercises

1. How could you best describe how the Buffaloes protect each other?

   A. Strength in numbers- they stick together
   B. Their spiky horns scare off predators
   C. Their size scares off predators
   D. They trick their predators

Re-read paragraphs 10 and 11.

4. What do you think the word timid most likely means?

   A. Happy
   B. Hungry
   C. Scared
   D. Sad

2. Why are the bull buffaloes in the front and back of the group?

   A. Some bull buffaloes want to drink first
   B. Bull buffaloes are the males and they protect the women and children in the middle
   C. Bull buffaloes test the water to make sure it's safe to drink
   D. Bull buffaloes do this so that the other buffaloes can hide

5. How does the deer get a drink?

   A. She hides in the rows of buffaloes, gets a drink, then hides in the bushes
   B. She gets a drink first, then hides in the rows of buffaloes
   C. She hides in the bushes, gets a drink then hides in the rows of buffaloes
   D. She hides in the buffaloes the whole time

3. What do buffaloes do when they are done with their turn drinking?

   A. Go back to the jungle
   B. Walk to the side and stay there to protect the others
   C. Walk to the side then to the back to face the jungle to protect others
   D. Walk directly to the back to protect others

6. Why did buffaloes start to drink and travel in rows?

   A. It is a faster way to travel
   B. It is the way they have always traveled for protection
   C. The tiger killed many buffaloes and traveling in rows is a form of protection
   D. It is easier to hunt in rows

Notes

Elephants Drink First—but Downstream

First let us watch the elephants as they come to the river through the gap in the jungle.

See! They come one at a time, one behind another; for the gap is not big enough for more than one at the same time. The elephant is so big that it can get through the jungle only in this way.

First come a number of bull elephants. They are the Papa elephants; you can always tell them by the huge tusks they have. The bulls come first, in case there are any enemies waiting to hurt their children; for then the bulls can drive off the enemies.

As each bull elephant comes through the gap, you see him turn to our right, which is down the stream—that is, the way the water flows. You see the first one walk along the bank that way, and the second comes after him, then the third, and so on.

But why do they walk along the bank? To make room, of course, for all their friends who are still coming from behind. In this way about a dozen bull elephants come ahead of all the others.

After them you see the cow elephants, also in a line, one behind another. They are the Mamma elephants; and nearly every one of them has a baby elephant trotting in front of her.

The Mamma elephant is wise, and always tells her baby to toddle in front of her, in case any one comes suddenly to hurt or steal the baby. For a tiger sometimes wants to pounce on the baby from the side, grab it quickly, and carry it away. But he cannot do it if the baby is right in front of its Mamma; for then she will drive him off with her tusks, even if they are not quite so big as the tusks that the Papa elephants have.

As the Mammas reach the bank, each with her baby, you see them also walk along the bank down stream in a long line.

After all the Mammas and babies have come, you see another set of bull elephants coming out of the jungle. Why? Because some enemy might try to attack the Mammas and the babies from the back; so these bull elephants are there to guard them. You see, the Mammas and the babies are always in the middle, safe from all harm.

When all the elephants have reached the stream, they stand in line and face the water. All these elephants belong to one herd; you can count about a hundred. A herd of elephants is really a republic, like the United States of America, and has a President, who is the wisest bull in the herd.

And in the jungle, as there are other elephant herds and sometimes two herds find the same feeding ground, and then start fighting as to who found it first, it is the duty of the President to keep his own herd away from the two that are fighting, and not mix in the fight in any way.

But let us see what the President has to do when the whole herd is standing in line, facing the water. He is at the bottom of the line, far downstream; so he looks up along the line to see that all are ready. Then he gives the signal for them to begin drinking; he does this by dipping his trunk into the water. Then the second one sees him do it, and does the same; in that way each elephant higher up the line sees that the next one below him has started drinking, so he too does the same. Soon they are all drinking.

But why does the President have to give the signal to begin? Why is it that any elephant, anywhere along the line, cannot start drinking, just as he or she pleases?

If any one along the line started drinking too soon, he might muddy the water for those that stood below him along the line, because the water flows down that way. But if the lower ones drank a little before, it

After reading the passage, read all answer choices for the question you are working on and then cross out the 2 that don't make sense.

would not matter if they did muddy the water, for the higher ones would still have clear water to drink. That is why the lowest one drinks first, then the next, and so on up the line. It is very wise, and very fair to all.

How the Elephant Drinks

But you must not think that an elephant actually drinks through his trunk! He does not! The elephant's trunk is really his nose, though it is a very long nose. What he does is to dip the trunk into the stream and suck in the water about halfway up the trunk; then he curls up the tip of the trunk and gets it near his mouth; then he blows through the nose, and squirts the water into his mouth. Of course he has to do that many times, to get enough to drink. But he tries each time to dip only the tip of the trunk into the stream, so as not to muddy the water willfully!

Why the Elephant Drinks with His Trunk

But, you may say, why cannot he drink like other animals, by going right into the stream till he gets his mouth into the water? Because his mouth is so high up, and his neck is so stiff, that he would have to go quite two or three yards deep into the stream before he could get his mouth into the water, and then his heavy feet would stir up the mud in the stream where he was standing, and so dirty the very water he was drinking.

Now you see what a wise animal the elephant is! The only way he could get clear water to drink was by having a long nose! And that is exactly what happened many, many years ago—his nose became long enough to reach the water from the bank.

Exercises

1. Why do the elephants walk in 1 row to the river?

   A. To make sure the water doesn't get muddy
   B. It is faster
   C. It makes hunting easier
   D. There is only room for one elephant at a time.

2. How do mother elephants protect their babies?

   A. They carry them
   B. The babies walk alongside of the mothers
   C. The babies walk in front of their mothers
   D. They babies walk in front of the pack of elephants

3. How do the elephants know when to drink water?

   A. They drink when they are thirsty
   B. The drink when the President dips his trunk in the water at the bottom of the line
   C. They drink when it is safe from predators
   D. The drink when the President dips his trunk in the water at the front of the line

4. What would happen if the elephants drank out of order?

   A. They would fight over who drank first
   B. The water would be muddy for others
   C. The President would be mad
   D. The elephants might get attacked

Re-read this sentence from the passage. "A herd of elephants is really a republic, like the United States of America, and has a President, who is the wisest bull in the herd."

5. What do you think the word republic means in this sentence?

   A. Democracy
   B. A large organized group of elephants
   C. A group of voters
   D. Angry elephants

6. How does the elephant drink water?

   A. His trunk helps him bring water to his mouth
   B. His nose is actually his mouth
   C. He bends down and sips from the water
   D. He drinks through his trunk

Notes

Benjamin Bunny

1.   One morning a little rabbit name Benjamin Bunny sat on a bank. He raised his ears and listened to the trit-trot, trit-trot of a pony. A carriage was coming along the road; it was driven by Mr. McGregor, and beside him sat Mrs. McGregor in her best hat.

2.   As soon as they had passed, little Benjamin Bunny slid down into the road, and set off—with a hop, skip, and a jump—to see his relatives, who lived in the woods at the back of Mr. McGregor's garden.

3.   Those woods were full of rabbit holes; and in the neatest, hole of all lived Benjamin's aunt and his cousins—Flopsy, Mopsy, Cotton-tail, and Peter. Old Mrs. Rabbit (his aunt) was a widow; she earned her living by knitting rabbit-wool mittens. She also sold herbs, and rosemary tea, and rabbit-tobacco (which is what we call lavender).

4.   Little Benjamin did not very much want to see his Aunt. He came round back and nearly tumbled upon the top of his Cousin Peter. Peter was sitting by himself. He looked poorly, and was dressed in nothing but a red cotton pocket-handkerchief.

5.   "Peter," said little Benjamin, in a whisper, "who has got your clothes?"

6.   Peter replied, "The scarecrow in Mr. McGregor's garden." He described how he had been chased about the garden, and had dropped his shoes and coat. Little Benjamin sat down beside his cousin and told him that Mr. McGregor had gone out in a carriage, and Mrs. McGregor also; and surely for the whole day, because she was wearing her best hat.

7.   At this point old Mrs. Rabbit's voice was heard inside the rabbit hole, calling: "Peter! Peter! Fetch some more herbs!"

8.   Peter said he thought he might feel better if he went for a walk. So, they went away hand in hand, and got on top the wall at the bottom of the woods. From here they looked down into Mr. McGregor's garden. Peter's coat and shoes were easy to see on the scarecrow, topped with an old hat of Mr. McGregor's.

9.   Little Benjamin said: "It spoils people's clothes to squeeze under a gate; the proper way to get in is to climb down the pear-tree."

10.   Peter fell down head first; but it was of no trouble as the bed below was quite soft. It had been made with lettuces. They left a great many odd little footmarks all over the bed, especially little Benjamin, who was wearing wooden clogs.

11.   Little Benjamin said that the first thing to be done was to get back Peter's clothes, so that they might be able to use the pocket-handkerchief Peter was wearing. They took them off the scarecrow. There had been rain during the night; there was water in the shoes, and the coat was somewhat shrunk. Then he suggested that they should fill the pocket-handkerchief with onions, as a little present for his Aunt.

12.   Peter did not seem to be enjoying himself; he kept hearing noises. Benjamin, on the contrary, was perfectly at home, and ate a lettuce leaf. He said that he was in the habit of coming to the garden with his father to get lettuces for their Sunday dinner.

13.   The lettuces certainly were very fine. Peter did not eat anything; he said he would like to go home. He dropped half the onions.

14.   Little Benjamin said that it was not possible to get back up the pear-tree with a load of vegetables. He led the way towards the other end of the garden. They went along a little walk under a sunny, red brick wall.

15.   Little Benjamin was a step or two in front of his cousin when he suddenly stopped. Little Benjamin took one look, and then, in half a minute or less, he hid himself and Peter and the onions underneath a large basket.

Truly understand what the questions are asking you by re-writing or restating them in your own words. It will make figuring out the answer easier.

16.   The cat got up and stretched herself, and came and sniffed at the basket. Perhaps she liked the smell of onions! Anyway, she sat down upon the top of the basket. She sat there for five hours.

17.   The cat looked up and saw old Mr. Benjamin Bunny (Benjamin's Dad) prancing along the top of the upper wall. He was smoking a pipe of rabbit-tobacco, and had a little switch in his hand. He was looking for his son. Old Mr. Bunny had no opinion whatever of cats.

18.   He took a tremendous jump off the top of the wall on to the top of the cat, and hit the cat off the basket, and kicked it into the greenhouse, scratching off a handful of fur.

19.   The cat was too much surprised to scratch back. When old Mr. Bunny had driven the cat into the greenhouse, he locked the door.

20.   Then he came back to the basket and took out his son Benjamin by the ears, and whipped him with the little switch. Then he took out his nephew Peter. Then he took out the handkerchief of onions, and marched out of the garden.

21.   When Mr. McGregor returned about half an hour later he saw several things, which confused and angered him. It looked as though some person had been walking all over the garden in a pair of clogs—only the footmarks were too ridiculously little! Also he could not understand how the cat could have managed to shut herself up inside the greenhouse, locking the door from the outside.

22.   When Peter got home his mother forgave him, because she was so glad to see that he had found his shoes and coat. Peter folded up the pocket-handkerchief, and old Mrs. Rabbit strung up the onions and hung them from the kitchen ceiling, with the bunches of herbs and the rabbit-tobacco.

Exercises

1. What do we learn about little Benjamin Bunny in paragraph 2?

   A. He loves his aunt
   B. He lives in the wood behind Mr. McGregor's house
   C. His relatives live in the woods behind Mr. McGregor's house
   D. He has good hearing

Re-read paragraph 12.

2. Why did Benjamin feel at home in the McGregor's garden?

   A. He had been there many times before with his father
   B. He lives there
   C. He knows that he is allowed in the garden
   D. His dad gave him permission

Re-read this phrase from the story, "He took a tremendous jump off the top of the wall on to the top of the cat..."

3. What do you think the word tremendous means in this phrase?

   A. Large
   B. Wonderful
   C. Lovely
   D. Small

4. Which best describes Peter?

   A. He is brave
   B. He is smart
   C. He is scared
   D. He is a leader

5. At the end of the story when Mr. McGregor comes home he sees that someone has been in his garden and he is angry. What are 2 reasons Mr. McGregor is angry? Use examples from the passage to support your answer.

6. In the story Peter and and Benjamin go to Mr. McGregor's garden. What are some of the things that Peter and Benjamin take from Mr. McGregor's garden? Name 2 things they take. Use examples from the passage to support your answer.

WEEK 5

VIDEO
EXPLANATIONS

ARGOPREP.COM

The Selfish Giant

1. Every afternoon, as they were coming from school, the children used to go and play in the Giant's garden.

2. It was a large lovely garden, with soft green grass. Over the grass stood beautiful flowers like stars, and there were twelve peach-trees. The birds sat on the trees and sang so sweetly that the children used to stop their games in order to listen to them. "How happy we are here!" they cried to each other.

3. One day the Giant came back. He had been to visit his friend the ogre, and had stayed with him for seven years. After the seven years were over he arrived he saw the children playing in the garden.

4. "What are you doing here?" he cried in a very gruff voice, and the children ran away. "My own garden is my own garden," said the Giant; "any one can understand that, and I will allow nobody to play in it but myself." So he built a high wall all round it, and put up a sign.
TRESPASSERS
WILL BE
PROSECUTED

5. He was a very selfish Giant. The poor children had now nowhere to play. They tried to play on the road, but the road was very dusty and full of hard stones, and they did not like it. They used to wander round the high wall when school was over, and talk about the beautiful garden inside. "How happy we were there!" they said to each other.

6. Then the Spring came, and all over the country there were little blossoms and little birds. Only in the garden of the Selfish Giant it was still winter. The birds did not care to sing in it as there were no children, and the trees forgot to blossom. Once a beautiful flower put its head out from the grass, but when it saw the sign, it was so sorry for the children that it slipped back into the ground again, and went off to sleep.

7. The only people who were pleased were the Snow and the Frost. "Spring has forgotten this garden," they cried, "so we will live here all the year round." The Snow covered up the grass with her great white and the Frost painted all the trees silver. Then they invited the North Wind to stay with them, and he came.

8. "This is a delightful spot," he said, "we must ask the Hail on a visit." So the Hail came. Every day for three hours he rattled on the roof of the castle till he broke most of the slates, and then he ran round and round the garden as fast as he could go. He was dressed in grey, and his breath was like ice.

9. "I cannot understand why the Spring is so late in coming," said the Selfish Giant, as he sat at the window and looked out at his cold white garden; "I hope there will be a change in the weather."

10. But the Spring never came, nor the Summer. The Autumn gave golden fruit to every garden, but to the Giant's garden she gave none. "He is too selfish," she said. So it was always Winter there, and the North Wind and the Hail, and the Frost, and the Snow danced about through the trees.

11. One morning the Giant was lying awake in bed when he heard some lovely music. "I believe the Spring has come at last," said the Giant; and he jumped out of bed and looked out.

12. He saw a most wonderful sight. Through a little hole in the wall the children had snuck in, and they were sitting in the branches of the trees. In every tree that he could see there was a little child. And the trees were so glad to have the children back again that they had covered themselves with flowers, and

Write a short summary or notes on the side of each paragraph or group of paragraphs so when you go back to find information in the text you know exactly where to go.

were waving their arms gently above the children's heads. The birds were flying about and twittering with delight, and the flowers were looking up through the green grass and laughing. It was a lovely scene, only in one corner it was still winter. It was the farthest corner of the garden, and in it was standing a little boy.

13. He was so small that he could not reach up to the branches of the tree, and he was wandering all round it, crying bitterly. The poor tree was still quite covered with frost and snow, and the North Wind was blowing and roaring above it. "Climb up! little boy," said the Tree, and it bent its branches down as low as it could; but the boy was too tiny. And the Giant's heart melted as he looked out. "How selfish I have been!" he said; "now I know why the Spring would not come here. I will put that poor little boy on the top of the tree, and then I will knock down the wall, and my garden shall be the children's playground for ever and ever."

Exercises

1. The giant puts up a sign that says "Trespassers will be Prosecuted." What do you think the sign means?

   A. People who enter the garden will be killed
   B. People who enter the garden will be in trouble with the law
   C. People who enter the garden must help work in the garden
   D. People may enter the garden

2. Why did the Spring stay away from the giant's garden?

   A. It was just a long winter
   B. The winter beat the spring in a fight
   C. The spring didn't like the giant
   D. The spring was sad there were no children in the garden

3. How do paragraphs 9 and 10 relate?

   A. Paragraph 9 shows the giant questioning what is happening and paragraph 10 shows why it is happening
   B. Paragraph 9 shows the cause of the giant's actions and paragraph 10 shows the effect
   C. Paragraph 9 explains why the giant acted this way and paragraph 10 shows how he did
   D. Paragraph 9 shows how the giant acted and paragraph 10 explains why he acted this way

4. How did Spring make its way back into the giant's garden?

   A. The giant broke down the wall to let spring in
   B. Spring had had enough of Winter so it broke down the giant's wall
   C. The boys convinced Spring to come back
   D. The boys snuck through a hole in the wall and spring came with them

5. Which statement best shows the theme of the story?

   A. With patience comes good things
   B. Selfishness should be met with selfishness
   C. Be kind to others and good things will happen
   D. A lesson learned is never good

6. Based on the story which best describes the Spring?

   A. Mean
   B. Selfish
   C. Wise
   D. Rude

Notes

The Emperor's New Suit

Many, many years ago lived an emperor, who thought so much of new clothes that he spent all his money in order to obtain them; his only wish was to be always well dressed. He did not care for his soldiers, and the theatre did not amuse him; the only thing, in fact, he thought anything of was to drive out and show a new suit of clothes.

One day two swindlers came to this city; they made people believe that they were clothes makers, and said they could make the finest cloth. Their colors and patterns, they said, were not only beautiful, but the clothes were made of material that made them invisible to any man who was not smart or good enough for the king.

"That must be wonderful cloth," thought the emperor. "If I were to be dressed in a suit made of this cloth I should be able to find out which men in my empire are not good enough for me, and I could tell the clever from the stupid. I must have this cloth woven for me without delay." And he gave a large sum of money to the swindlers. They set up two looms, and pretended to be very hard at work, but they did nothing whatever on the looms. They asked for the finest silk and the most precious gold-cloth; they kept all of the materials.

"I should very much like to know how the clothes makers are doing with the cloth," thought the emperor. But he felt rather uneasy when he remembered that only smart people could see the cloth.

"I shall send my honest old minister to the weavers," thought the emperor."

The good old minister went into the room where the swindlers sat before the empty looms. "I cannot see anything at all," but he did not say so. Both swindlers asked him to come near, and asked him if he did not like the pattern and the beautiful colours, pointing to the empty looms. The poor old minister tried his very best, but he could see nothing, for there was nothing to be seen.

"Oh dear," he thought, "can I be so stupid?

"Now, have you got nothing to say?" said one of the swindlers, while he pretended to be busily weaving.

"Oh, it is very pretty, exceedingly beautiful," replied the old minister looking through his glasses. "What a beautiful pattern, what brilliant colours! I shall tell the emperor that I like the cloth very much."

"We are pleased to hear that," said the two weavers.

Now the swindlers asked for more money and silk and gold-cloth, which they required for weaving. They kept everything for themselves, and not a thread came near the looms. The emperor sent more men to check on the cloth, and although none of them saw the cloth, they all told the emperor how amazing it was!

Everybody in the whole town talked about the precious cloth. At last the emperor wished to see it himself, while it was still on the loom. With a number of men, including some who had already been there, he went to the two clever swindlers, who now worked as hard as they could, but without using any thread.

"Is it not magnificent?" said the two old men who had been there before. And then they pointed to the empty looms, for they imagined the others could see the cloth.

"What is this?" thought the emperor, "I do not see anything at all. That is terrible! Am I stupid? Am I unfit to be emperor? That would indeed be the most dreadful thing that could happen to me."

"It is very beautiful," said the emperor. And all the men told him to wear the new magnificent clothes at a great parade which was soon to take place.

The emperor and all his men then came to a hall; the swindlers held their arms up as if they held something in their hands and said: "These are the pants!" "This is the coat!" and "Here is the cloak!" and so

The longest part of this assignment and the actual test is reading! Take your time when reading the passages and use whatever strategies you are comfortable with.

on. "They are all as light as a cobweb, and one must feel as if one had nothing at all upon the body; but that is just the beauty of them."

"Indeed!" said all the men; but they could not see anything, for there was nothing to be seen.

The emperor undressed, and the swindlers pretended to put the new suit upon him, one piece after another; and the emperor looked at himself in the glass from every side.

"How well they look! How well they fit!" said all. "What a beautiful pattern! What fine colours! That is a beautiful suit of clothes!"

"I am ready," said the emperor. "Does not my suit fit me perfectly?"

The emperor marched in the parade and all who saw him in the street and out of the windows exclaimed: "What a perfect suit!" Nobody wished to let others know they saw nothing, for then he would have been thought of as too stupid.

"But he has nothing on at all," said a little child at last. "Good heavens! listen to the voice of a child," said the father, and one whispered to the other what the child had said. "But he has nothing on at all," cried at last the whole people. That made a deep impression upon the emperor, for it seemed to him that they were right; but he thought to himself, "Now I must continue this up to the end." And the men walked with still greater importance right by the emperor's side.

Exercises

1. Which best shows how the swindlers described the cloth for the emperor?

A. Only the person wearing the cloth could see it
B. Only those smart enough to see the cloth could see it
C. Only those who were loyal enough could see it
D. Only the emperor could see the cloth

2. What do you think the word swindler most likely means?

A. People who makes clothes
B. People who grew up in a different city
C. People who trick and rob others
D. People who are nice and helpful

3. Why did the emperor send men to look at the cloth before he went to see it himself?

A. He wanted to make sure it was as beautiful as the swindlers said it would be
B. He was nervous about not being able to see the cloth so he sent men to check it out first
C. He was too important to check on other's work
D. He was too busy with other things

4. Which two words best describe the emperor's men?

A. Stupid and loyal
B. Caring and stupid
C. Loyal and concerned
D. Concerned and stupid

5. Why doesn't anyone tell the emperor there are no clothes?

A. They fear his punishment
B. They fear they are too stupid to see the clothes
C. They fear the swindlers
D. They hate the emperor and like tricking him

6. Which best shows the main theme from the story?

A. Don't be greedy or you'll be tricked others who aren't as wealthy
B. Tell the truth even if you're scared others won't believe you or will think you're stupid
C. Always trust a child's thoughts
D. Don't trust strangers because they'll always trick you

Notes

A Boy's Heroic Deeds

1. May 31st, 1889, is a day that will long be remembered with horror by the people in the beautiful valley of the Conemaugh, in Pennsylvania. On that date the terrible disaster which is known to the world and will be named in history as the "Johnstown Flood."

2. For many days before it had been raining hard, and great floods extended over a large region of country in Pennsylvania, New York and the District of Columbia. Never before had there been such a fall of rain in that region.

3. The waters in the river and creeks of that beautiful valley rose quickly and overflowed their banks, while the people looked on in wonder, but seemingly not in fear. Suddenly a man riding a horse appeared who waved his hands to them and cried: "South Fork dam will burst. To the hills for your lives."

4. Only a few listened to his words of warning, while many mocked and jeered. On went the horse rider to warn others of the danger, and, alas, he was killed along with his horse by a falling bridge.

5. South Fork dam did break, and the mighty waters of Conemaugh Lake were thrown with great force upon the doomed people of that beautiful valley. The terrible details of the disaster would fill many pages larger than this.

6. On rushed the mighty waters, destroying houses, churches and buildings of every description, whether of wood, brick or stone, until Johnstown was destroyed. The town was literally lifted from its foundations.

7. Thousands of men, women and children were caught up and taken away in the flood.

8. Many acts of heroism were performed by brave men and women—yes, and boys—in rescuing victims of the flood. Only one of them concerns us here. Charles Hepenthal, a schoolboy, seventeen years of age, who was on his way home on the evening of the flood, stood quietly among the passengers on the express train, as they crowded to view the terrible damage done by the flood. As the flood reached the train, at Sang Hollow, a small house came rushing down the tide, near to the train, so close that the cries of an infant were heard, making their way above the roar of the water and the train.

9. Charles Hepenthal's heart was touched and his courage was equal to the emergency. He determined to rescue that little crying baby from a watery grave. Strong men urged him not to go, telling him that he would only sacrifice his own life for nothing—that it was impossible for anyone to survive in the waters.

10. But the boy was determined. He cut the bell cord from the cars, tied it fast to his body, and out into the whirling waters he went; he reached the house, secured the infant and returned through the maddened waters with the rescued babe in his arms.

11. A shout went up from the passengers on the train. "Wait!" he cried; "there is still another in the house, I must save her!" and, grabbing a piece of wood to use as a support, he plunged again into the surging waters.

12. Ah! his struggle this time was harder, for his precious load was heavy. In the floating house he found a little girl, apparently ten years old, kneeling beside her bed. In another minute she would have been drowned. But the brave boy's manly arms were soon around her, and with his precious load the young hero fought his way back to land and was given three times three cheers and a "hoo-ray" by the passengers of the day express train.

TIP of the DAY

When reading think about the author's purpose not just for the entire passage but for individual paragraphs or sections of information. Why would they include this information? What purpose does it serve?

Exercises

Re-read paragraph 1.

1. Why do you think the author begins the passage this way?

    A. To tell the reader how the Johnstown flood started
    B. To tell the reader why the flood started
    C. To tell the reader what they will be reading about
    D. To tell the reader who the hero was in the story

Re-read this phrase from the passage. "Only a few listened to his words of warning, while many mocked and jeered."

3. What do you think the phrase mocked and jeered means?

    A. Ran and screamed
    B. Fought and cried
    C. Got worried and talked about it
    D. Made fun of him and laughed at him

2. Why do you think the author included the story about the horse rider?

    A. To entertain the reader while reading about an old event
    B. To show that people didn't think the flood was going to be a big deal
    C. To show how people traveled back in the day
    D. To help give you a visual of the event

4. How did the boy survive in the waters when he went to save the baby?

    A. He asked the other passengers for help
    B. He used his strength to fight over the waters
    C. He cut a cord and tied it to himself so he wouldn't get washed away
    D. He used a piece of wood to support him

Exercises

5. Many horrible things happened during the Johnstown flood. What caused the Johnstown flood? Describe 2 things that caused the Johnstown flood to occur. Use details from the text to support your answer.

6. What kind of person is Charles Hepenthal? Give 2 reasons to back up your claim. Use details from the text to support your answer.

WEEK 6

VIDEO
EXPLANATIONS

ARGOPREP.COM

Dan, the Newsboy an excerpt from chapter 1, **Introducing Dan**

1. "Evening Telegram! Only one left. Going for two cents, and worth double the money. Buy one, sir?"
2. Attracted by the business-like tone of the newsboy, a gentleman paused as he was walking up the steps of the Astor House, and said, with a smile:
3. "You seem to like the Telegram, my boy. Any important news this afternoon?"
4. "Buy the paper, and you'll see," said the boy, quickly.
5. "I see—you don't care to part with the news for nothing. Well, here are your two cents."
6. "Thank you, sir."
7. "How many papers have you sold to-day, my boy?" he asked.
8. "Thirty-six, sir."
9. "Were they all Telegrams?"
10. "No; I sell all the papers. I ain't partial. I'm just as willing to make money on the Mail, or Commercial, or Evening Post, as the Telegram."
11. "I see you have an eye to business. How long have you dealt in papers?"
12. "Three years, sir."
13. "How old are you?"
14. "Fifteen."
15. "What did you do before you sold papers?"
16. A shadow rested on the boy's bright face.
17. "I didn't have to work then, sir," he said. "My father was alive, and he was well off. We lived in a nice house up town, and I went to a private school. But all at once father failed, and soon afterward he died, and then everything was changed. I don't like to think about it, sir."
18. The gentleman's interest was strongly excited.
19. "It is a sad story," he said. "Is your mother living?"
20. "Yes, sir. The worst of it is, that I don't make enough to support us both, and she has to work, too."
21. "What does she do?"
22. "She makes vests for a man on Chatham street."
23. "I hope she is well paid."
24. "That she is not. He only allows her twenty cents a piece."
25. "That is nothing. She can't earn much at that rate."
26. "No, sir; she has to work hard to make one vest a day."
27. "The man can't have a heart," said the gentleman, in an upset tone. "It is starvation wages."
28. "So it is, sir, but he pretends that he pays more than the work is worth. Oh, he's a mean fellow,"said the boy, his face full of the scorn and disgust which he felt.
29. "What is your name, my boy?"
30. "Dan, sir—Dan Mordaunt."
31. "I hope, Dan, you make more money than your mother does."
32. "Oh, yes, sir. Sometimes I make a dollar a day, but I don't average that. I wish I could make enough so that mother wouldn't have to work."
33. "I see you are a good son. I like to hear you speak in such terms of your mother."

If you are stuck on a question, skip it, don't stress! Move on to the next one. Before you start the next passage go back and answer the question you left blank.

34. "If I didn't," said Dan, "I should deserve to be kicked. She's a good mother, sir."
35. "I have no doubt of it. It must be hard for her to have to work so hard after once living such a nice life. How happened it that your father failed?"
36. The boy's kind face made a stern look.
37. "On account of a rascal, sir. His book-keeper ran off, carrying with him thirty thousand dollars. Father couldn't meet his bills, and so he failed. It broke his heart, and he didn't live six months after it."
38. "Have you ever heard of this book-keeper since?"
39. "No, sir, not a word. I wish I could. I should like to see him dragged to prison, for he killed myfather, and made my mother work for a living."
40. "I can't blame you, Dan, for feeling as you do. It has changed your life."
41. "I don't care for myself, sir. I can forget that. But I can't forgive the injury he has done my poor father and mother."

Exercises

Re-read lines 7-10.

1. What does the phrase "I ain't partial" mean in the sentence, "No; I sell all the papers. I ain't partial"?

    A. I don't do half my job
    B. I don't have a favorite to sell
    C. I'm not working part time
    D. I'm not rich

2. What does the gentleman learn about the boy in paragraph 17?

    A. How he likes his job
    B. Why his mother is working
    C. How he became a newsboy
    D. His father had died

3. Which statement best shows how the gentleman felt about the boy?

    A. He thinks the boy should treat his mother better
    B. He thinks the boy should work harder to make more money
    C. He thinks the boy is a good son for working hard for his mother
    D. He thinks nothing of the boy

4. Which statement best describes the boy?

    A. He works hard because he likes to sell the papers
    B. He is nice to the gentleman because he wants his money
    C. He works hard to help support his mother
    D. He is happy his mother has a job

5. Which statement best describes the gentleman?

    A. He is upset because he knew the boy's father
    B. He is upset because he wishes he could get the paper cheaper
    C. He is happy he met such a fine young boy
    D. He thinks it is unfair that the boy's mother makes so little money

Re-read paragraph 37.

6. How did the boy's father die?

    A. He was killed by a burglar, who took money from him
    B. He died of a broken heart, his heart actually broke
    C. After he was robbed, he couldn't pay his bills and he became sick and died, probably from the stress
    D. Someone, stole all of his money so he couldn't afford medicine when his heart broke

Notes

Find detailed video explanations to each problem on: **ArgoPrep.com**

Queen Margaret and the Robbers

1. There were once two kings of England at the same time. One was Henry VI. He was the rightful king, but a very weak and feeble man, and quite unfit to rule his kingdom.

2. The other was young Edward, Duke of York, called Edward IV. He was made king by some of the nobles, who grew weary of Henry and his foolish deeds.

3. A number of the English people were faithful to King Henry, but many others went over to King Edward's side, and there were fights between the two parties, which ended in a war. This war was called the War of the Roses, because the followers of Henry wore a red rose as their badge, and Edward's friends wore a white one.

4. In one battle, fought at Hexham, the White Roses beat the Red ones, and King Henry was taken prisoner and sent to the Tower of London. His wife, Queen Margaret, with her little son, Prince Edward, escaped after the battle, and hid themselves in a wild forest.

5. As they wandered among the trees, seeking some place where they might be safe from their enemies, they met a band of robbers. These rough men took away the queen's money and her jewels, tearing her necklace from her neck, and her rings from her fingers.

6. Then the robbers began to argue as to who should have most of the stolen goods. And while they fought, Queen Margaret took her little boy by the hand and ran away to a thick part of the wood. There they stayed until the angry voices of the robbers could no longer be heard, and then, in the growing darkness, they came sneakily from their hiding-place.

7. They wandered on, knowing not where to go, hoping much to meet some of their friends, and fearing still more to be found by their enemies, the soldiers of the White Rose. But, alas! they saw no kind face, and night came on. Then, as they crept fearfully from tree to tree, they met another robber.

8. The poor queen was much afraid that this robber, who looked very mad, would kill her and the prince, because she had no riches left to give him. In despair she threw herself upon her knees before him, and said: "My friend, this is the son of your king. I give him into your care." The robber was much surprised to see the queen and the prince alone, with their clothes torn and stained, and their faces white from hunger and fatigue.

9. But he was a kind hearted man, although his looks were rough, and before he became a robber he had been a follower of King Henry, so he was quite willing to do his best for the little prince. He took the boy in his arms, and led the way to a cave in the forest, where he lived with his wife. And in this poor shelter, the queen and her son stayed for two days, listening to every sound, and fearing that their enemies would find them.

10. On the third day, however, the friendly robber met some of the lords of the Red Rose in the forest, and led them to the cave. The queen and prince were overjoyed to see their friends, and soon they escaped with them to a place of safety.

11. Their hiding-place has been called "Queen Margaret's Cave" ever since that time. If you go to Hexham Forest, you will be able to see it.

  *Even for multiple choice answers you should be able to back up your answer choice with evidence from the text. Prove your answer is correct by using this strategy.*

Exercises

1. Which best describes the War of the Roses?

  A. King Henry's friends wore a red rose and fought against King Edward's friends who wore a white rose
B. King Henry's friends wore a white rose and fought against King Edward's friends who wore a red rose
C. King Henry and King Edward fought over which color rose should represent the kingdom
D. King Henry and King Edward fought over robbers who were in the kingdom

Re-read paragraph 2.

2. What do you think the word weary means in this sentence?

  A. Angry
B. Tired
C. Excited
D. Surprised

3. Which statement best describes how Queen Margaret and Prince Edward were robbed?

  A. King Edward's men robbed them of their goods
B. After the war, the Queen and the Prince escaped but were robbed of their goods first
C. After the war, the Queen and the Prince escaped to the woods and were found by robbers
D. The Queen and the Prince were robbed by men with roses

4. What do we learn about the second robber in paragraph 9?

  A. He was interested in robbing the Queen and the Prince
B. He was not a smart man, he got tricked by the Queen and the Prince
C. He was a friend of King Henry and did not want to hurt the Queen or the Prince
D. He was a friend of King Edward and did not want to hurt the Queen or the Prince

5. Which sentence best describes the Queen?

  A. She is smart, quick, and witty because she escaped from trouble more than once
B. She is not very smart because she keeps getting in trouble
C. She is lucky she has the prince to protect her
D. She is lucky because she keeps escaping

6. Which sentence best shows how paragraph 8 relates to paragraph 9?

  A. Paragraph 8 explains why robber was mad and paragraph 9 shows his reaction to being mad
B. In paragraph 8 the robber explains why he is robbing them and paragraph 9 shows how sorry he is
C. Paragraph 8 shows how the Queen tries to stop the robber and paragraph 9 shows the robber's reaction and decision
D. Paragraph 8 shows how the Queen and the robber argue and paragraph 9 shows what he does

Wild Dogs in India

1. By Wild Dogs, we mean true dogs, that in different parts of the world are found living in a wild state; and also Wolves, Foxes, Jackals, and Hyenas—for all these are but dogs in a state of nature.

2. First, we shall speak of the true dogs living in a wild state—that is, dogs that live away from man.

3. It is not needed here to go into the often-debated question, as to whether dogs were originally wolves, or what species of wolf the dog comes from. This is all educated guessing, and answers no purpose. It is just as likely that wolves came from dogs, as that dogs came from wolves. Foxes differ only from wolves in point of size; and a small wolf is really a fox, while a large fox may be equally regarded as a wolf. Furthermore, the jackal is nothing else than another form of the same animal—the wolf or dog, whichever you choose to term it; and the hyenas but a still uglier shape of the same creature.

4. True wild dogs—which are not regarded as wolves—we find them existing in different parts of the world. They usually live in communities, and have the habit of hounds—that is, they hunt in packs. Whether they were first dogs in a domesticated state, and have since left from the home of man, is a question which scientists are unable to agree upon.

5. In India there are three kinds of wild dogs. One is the Deccan—a reddish-colored animal, nearly as large as the common European wolf. It lives in the forests, far away from the villages—and of course lives by preying upon other animals—just as wolves and foxes do.

6. In the forests of the Himalaya mountains (in India) there is another species of wild dog, different from that of the Deccan. It is usually known as the wild dog of Nepaul, from its being found in many parts of that kingdom. A large community of these animals often live within the mountain forests—living in caves, or at the bottoms of cliffs, where there are deep holes among the boulders of loose rocks, that give them a safe hiding when chased by their enemies. In these places the dogs sleep, and raise their young; and the puppies are taught to be very careful, and not stray far from their dens while their mothers are gone.

7. During the many hours the mothers and fathers of the wild dogs are gone, they are mostly hunting. They hunt in packs. This is the best way to hunt for them, as they can chase down prey from all different directions. An interesting fact is that when the wolves or wild dogs hunt bigger animals they trick them to coming close to their dens, so that they don't have to carry their kill as far. These are very smart animals. A fact seems to confirm it: the fact that a large number of bones of large animals is always found in the neighbourhood of the dens proves this to be true.

8. In Ramghur there is a wild dog called Quao, or Quaw, which lives in communities, just as those of Nepaul; and still another kind inhabits the forests of the Island of Sumatra.

9. None of these kinds are to be confused with the half-wild dogs of India, called pariah dogs. These dogs are not owned by people, but live on the streets in the villages, and of course associate with man. Besides, the pariahs are of no particular breed—there being several sorts of pariah dogs. They are without owners, that pick up a living as they best can.

Use the notes page to organize information for open response answers. Creating a list may take an extra minute or two now, but may save you time when writing your short response.

Exercises

1. Why do you think the author included information in paragraph 3 about where dogs come from?

   A. To show how dogs, wolves, foxes and others are different
   B. To explain that there is no real evidence to prove where dogs came from
   C. To explain how we found out where dogs came from
   D. To show why it is important to understand the differences between dogs and wolves

3. Which statement is most important to summarize the story?

   A. Dogs are not wolves but they do act the same sometimes
   B. We don't know where wild dogs come from, but they hunt in packs just like wolves
   C. Wild dogs are cool and interesting
   D. Some dogs live on the street in India

Re-read this sentence from paragraph 4. "Whether they were first dogs in a domesticated state, and have since left from the home of man, is a question which scientists are unable to agree upon."

2. What do you think the word domesticated means?

   A. Lived in the wild
   B. Lived in a home with people
   C. Unhealthy
   D. Hungry

4. Which statement shows that wild dogs trick their larger prey to come closer to their dens before killing them?

   A. Large bones can be found around the dens of wild dogs
   B. Scientists have watched this happen for themselves
   C. The young wait in the dens
   D. The mothers go out hunting to bring back food

5. There are 3 types of wild dogs in India, the Deccan, the wild dog of Nepaul and the Quao or Quaw. How are any of these dogs similar? Give 2 examples of how they are similar. Make sure to use details from the text to support your answer.

6. Wild dogs hunt in many ways. Describe 2 of the ways that wild dogs hunt. Be sure to include at least 2 examples. Make sure to use details from the text to support your answer.

WEEK 7

VIDEO
EXPLANATIONS

ARGOPREP.COM

The Landlord's Mistake

1. When John Adams was president and Thomas Jefferson was vice president of the United States, there was not a railroad in all the world.

2. People did not travel very much. There were no broad, smooth highways as there are now. The roads were crooked and muddy and rough.

3. If a man needed to go from one city to another, he often rode on horseback. Instead of a trunk for his clothing, he carried a pair of saddlebags. Instead of sitting in comfort in a parlor car, he went jolting along through mud and mire, exposed to wind and weather.

4. One day some men were sitting by the door of a hotel in Baltimore. As they looked down the street they saw a horseman coming. He was riding very slowly, and both he and his horse were bespattered with mud.

5. "There comes old Farmer Mossback," said one of the men, laughing. "He's just in from the backwoods."

6. "He seems to have had a hard time of it," said another; "I wonder where he'll put up for the night."

7. "Oh, any kind of a place will suit him," answered the landlord. "He's one of those country fellows who can sleep in the hay and eat with the horses."

8. The man was soon at the door. He was dressed plainly, and, with his reddish-brown hair and mud bespattered face, looked like a hard-working countryman just in from the back woods.

9. "Have you a room here for me?" he asked the landlord.

10. Now the landlord prided himself upon keeping a first-class hotel, and he feared that his guests would not like the rough-looking traveler. So he answered: "No, sir. Every room is full. The only place I could put you would be in the barn."

11. "Well, then," answered the stranger, "I will see what they can do for me at the Planters' Tavern, round the corner;" and he rode away.

12. About an hour later, a well-dressed gentleman came into the hotel and said, "I wish to see Mr. Jefferson."

13. "Mr. Jefferson!" said the landlord.

14. "Yes, sir. Thomas Jefferson, the vice president of the United States."

15. "He isn't here."

16. "Oh, but he must be. I met him as he rode into town, and he said that he intended to stop at this hotel. He was here about an hour."

17. "No, he hasn't. The only man that has been here for a room to-day was an old horseman who was so spattered with mud that you couldn't see the color of his coat. I sent him round to the Planters'."

18. "Did he have reddish-brown hair, and did he ride a gray horse?"

19. "Yes, and he was quite tall."

20. "That was Mr. Jefferson," said the gentleman.

21. "Mr. Jefferson!" cried the landlord. "Was that the vice president? Here, Hank! build a fire in the best room. Put everything in tiptop order, Sally. What a fool I was to turn Mr. Jefferson away! He shall have all the rooms in the house, and the ladies' parlor, too, I'll go right round to the Planters' and fetch him back."

22. So he went to the other hotel, where he found the vice president sitting with some friends in the parlor.

23. "Mr. Jefferson," he said, "I have come to ask for your forgiveness. You were so bespattered with mud that I thought you were some old farmer. If you'll come back to my house, you shall have the best room

 **TIP** of the **DAY**

Write SWBST on the side of the passage. Somebody, Wanted, But, So, Then. This can help keep track of information. This is the perfect passage to try that strategy. But remember, only use strategies that will help you!

init—yes, all the rooms if you wish. Won't you come?"

24. "No," answered Mr. Jefferson. "A farmer is as good as any other man; and where there's no room for a farmer, there can be no room for me."

Exercises

1. Which sentence best describes the landlord?

A. He is a kind man who just doesn't want to dirty his hotel
B. He is a judgemental man who doesn't give people a fair chance
C. He is a hardworking man who doesn't allow strangers in his hotel
D. He is a whining man who doesn't like the President or Vice President

Re-read paragraphs 1, 2 and 3.

2. Why do you think the author included this information in the passage?

A. To entertain us with a story from the past
B. To persuade us that we should be lucky to have cars now
C. To inform us of what life was like when the story took place
D. To persuade us that horseback was the best way to travel

3. Which sentence best describes how the landlord knew he had made a mistake?

A. The landlord realized it was Mr. Jefferson right after he left and ran after him to the next hotel
B. Someone came looking for Mr. Jefferson and described what he looked like, then the landlord realized who he turned away
C. Someone told the landlord that Mr. Jefferson had come into his hotel and he accidentally turned him away, and now he was in trouble
D. The landlord knew he made a mistake when Mr. Jefferson looked like the Vice President

Re-read paragraph 21.

4. Why is this paragraph important to the story?

A. It shows the landlord trying to fix his mistake
B. It explains why the landlord turned Mr. Jefferson away
C. It explains how he figured out who the man on horseback was
D. It shows that the landlord didn't feel bad about his mistake

5. Which statement best reflects the theme of this story?

A. Don't be greedy, or you'll pay in the end
B. Treat others the way you want to be treated
C. Don't judge a book by it's cover
D. Never turn a stranger away

6. Which statement best shows why Mr. Jefferson refused the landlord's offer at the end of the story?

A. He was very mad that he was turned away at first
B. He was very upset that he was turned away and didn't want to go back
C. He thought the landlord should let any person stay at his hotel, no matter how they looked
D. The other hotel was nicer

The Whisperers

1.   "Boys, what did I tell you?"

2.   The schoolmaster spoke angrily. He was upset because his students would not study. Whenever his back was turned, they were sure to begin whispering to one another.

3.   "Girls, stop your whispering, I say."

4.   But still they would whisper, and he could not prevent it. The afternoon was half gone, and the trouble was growing. Then the master thought of a plan.

5.   "Children," he said, "we are going to play a new game. The next one that whispers must come out and stand in the middle of the floor. He must stand there until he sees someone else whisper. Then he will tell me, and the one whom he names must come and take his place. He, in turn, will watch and report the first one that he sees whisper. And so we will keep the game going till it istime for school to be dismissed. The boy or girl who is standing at that time will be punished for all of you."

6.   "What will the punishment be, Mr. Johnson?" asked a bold, bad boy. "A good thrashing, "answered the master. He was tired, he was vexed, he hardly knew what he said.

7.   The children thought the new game was very funny. First, Tommy Jones whispered to Billy Brown and was at once called out to stand on the floor. Within less than two minutes, Billy saw Mary Green whispering, and she had to take his place. Mary looked around and saw Samuel Miller asking his neighbor for a pencil, and Samuel was called. And so the fun went on until the clock showed that it lacked only ten minutes till school would be dismissed.

8.   Then all became very good and very careful, for no one wished to be standing at the time of dismissal. They knew that the master would be as good as his word. The clock ticked loudly, and Tommy Jones, who was standing up for the fourth time, began to feel very uneasy. He stood on one leg and then on the other, and watched very closely; but nobody whispered.

9.   Could it be possible that he would receive that thrashing? Suddenly, to his great joy he saw little Lucy Martin lean over her desk and whisper to the girl in front of her. Now Lucy was the pet of the school. Everybody loved her, and this was the first time she had whispered that day. But Tommy didn't care for that. He wished to escape the punishment, and so he called out, "Lucy Martin!" and went proudly to his seat.

10.   Little Lucy had not meant to whisper. There was something which she wished very much to know before going home, and so, without thinking, she had leaned over and whispered just three littlewords. With tears in her eyes she went out and stood in the whisperer's place.

11.   She was very much ashamed and hurt, for it was the first time that she had ever been in disgrace at school. The other girls felt sorry that she should suffer for so small a fault. The boys looked at her and wondered if the master would really be as good as his word.

12.   The clock kept on ticking. It lacked only one minute till the bell would strike the time for dismissal. What a shame that dear, gentle Lucy should be punished for all those unruly boys and girls!

13.   Then, suddenly, an awkward half-grown boy who sat right in front of the master's desk turned squarely around and whispered to Tommy Jones, three desks away.

14.   Everybody saw him. Little Lucy Martin saw him through her tears, but said nothing. Everybody was astonished, for that boy was the best student in the school, and he had never been known to break a rule.

Re-read tricky questions or parts of the passage multiple times to help with understanding. You may find clues in the words and phrases surrounding the tricky part.

15. Only half a minute now until the day was over. The awkward boy turned again and whispered so loudly that even the master could not help hearing: "Tommy, you deserve a thrashing!"

16. "Elihu Burritt, take your place on the floor," said the master sternly. The awkward boy stepped out quickly, and little Lucy Martin returned to her seat sobbing. At the same moment the bellstruck and school was dismissed.

17. After all the others had gone home, the master took down his long birch rod and said: "Elihu, I suppose I must be as good as my word. But tell me why you so deliberately broke the rule against whispering."

18. "I did it to save little Lucy," said the awkward boy, standing up very straight and brave. "I could not bear to see her punished."

19. "Elihu, you may go home," said the master.

20. All this happened many years ago in New Britain, Connecticut. Elihu Burritt was a poor boy who was determined to learn. He worked many years as a blacksmith and studied books whenever he had a spare moment. He learned many languages and became known all over the world as "The Learned Blacksmith."

Exercises

1. How does paragraph 4 relate to paragraph 5?

   A. Paragraph 4 shows what the schoolmaster does to the children who whisper and paragraph 5 explains why he came up with this plan

   B. Paragraph 4 shows that the schoolmaster is angry at all the whispering and paragraph 5 explains his plan to stop it

   C. Paragraph 4 and 5 both show his feelings toward the children who whisper

   D. Paragraph 4 and 5 both explain why the children are whispering

2. Which statement best describes an effect of the schoolmaster's plan?

   A. The kids stopped whispering
   B. The kids whispered even more
   C. The kids thought the schoolmaster was funny
   D. The kids all got in trouble

3. Which sentence best describes why Elihu loudly whispers, "Tommy, you deserve a thrashing!" in paragraph 15?

   A. He hates Tommy
   B. He thinks it is unfair that Lucy got in trouble for whispering once when Tommy whispered many times, so he said it loudly so Lucy wouldn't get in trouble and he could take her place
   C. He thinks it is an unfair game and Tommy cheated, so he says this loudly so the schoolmaster could hear and punish Tommy not Lucy
   D. He was just joking with Tommy

4. Which two words best describe Elihu?

   A. Smart and Funny
   B. Coward and Mean
   C. Brave and Kind
   D. Dumb and Rude

5. Why does the schoolmaster let Elihu go home without punishment?

   A. He just wanted to scare the kids and not actually hit them
   B. He was proud of Elihu for standing up for Lucy
   C. Tommy is the smartest kid in the class
   D. He let him off with a warning

6. Which sentence best describes the schoolmaster throughout the whole story?

   A. He is frustrated at his class for whispering, so he comes up with a plan to hit the kid who whispers last in class, and he is a man of his word and angrily hits the last kid standing
   B. He is frustrated at his class for whispering, so he comes up with a plan to hit the kid who whispers last in class, but he was only kidding and said all of this just to scare the kids
   C. He is frustrated at his class for whispering, so he comes up with a plan to trick the kid who whispers last in class, he makes the last kid stay after, but lets him go after making him promise to tell the other kids he got hit, even when he didn't
   D. He is frustrated at his class for whispering, so he comes up with a plan to hit the kid who whispers last in class, but a boy stands up for a girl who whispers last and escapes punishment because the schoolmaster knows the boy did the right thing

Notes

 Find detailed video explanations to each problem on:
ArgoPrep.com

The First English Colony in America

1. In the beginning of the rule of James the First, the first successful attempt was made by the English to start a colony in America.

2. Three small ships, under the command of Captain Newport, formed the first unit that was to create a colony; and sailed with a hundred and five men destined to remain in America.

3. Several of these men were members of important English families including George Percy (royalty), Bartholomew Gosnald, the navigator, and Captain John Smith, one of the most important men of this time, who acted as Newport's co-captain.

4. Before Captain Newport's expedition, there had been an expedition to the New World to try and start a colony. Raleigh, in now what is North Carolina was the first try for the English to start a colony in the New World, but it failed. Now with a much smaller crew, Newport had a more difficult job trying to become friendly with the natives and learn the land.

5. Newport and his men did not finish their voyage in less than four months; the journey's end came due to the effect of a storm, which did not allow them to land and settle at Roanoak, but carried them into the bay of Chesapeak; and coasting along its southern shore, they entered a river which the natives called Powhatan, and explored its banks for more than forty miles.

6. The adventurers, impressed with the advantages of the coast and region determined to make this the place of their colony.

7. They gave to their new settlement, as well as the river, the name of their king; and Jamestown has the honor of being the oldest of existing colony of the English in America.

8. Newport landed the colonists with supplies that were going to last until their ship set sail to return to England, in the month of June, 1607.

9. The colonists soon found themselves limited to a scanty supply goods; and the heat, combining with the effect of their poor diet, brought on diseases that were deadly and caused men to fight.

10. Before the month of September, one half of their number had miserably died, and among these victims was Bartholomew Gosnald, who had planned the expedition, and greatly contributed to its success.

11. This scene of death was made worse by all of the fighting amongst the colonists. The sense of urgent danger, led them to listen to the advice of their leader, Captain John Smith. Every eye was now turned on Captain Smith, whose talents and experience. Some loved Smith, some were jealous of his power.

12. Under Captain Smith's directions, Jamestown was made strong by building a fort so they could fight off the the attacks of the savages, and the colonists and friendly natives were provided with house-like structures that gave shelter from the weather and helped improve their health.

13. Smith and his men were running out of supplies. So he gathered some of his men and went deep into the country where he found many natives to be kind and helpful. But, in the middle of this successful mission, he was attacked by an angry group of natives who took him prisoner.

14. Smith used his charm and wisdom to outsmart the tribe that had captured him. He asked to speak to the chief of the tribe and offered him a gift of a compass, something that the natives had never seen before. They were quite amazed at this instrument.

15. The savages listened to him with amazement. They handled the compass, viewing with surprise the play of the needle, which they plainly saw, but were unable to touch; and he appeared to have gained some trust over their minds.

  *Re-read your short answer responses to make sure you have answered the question, your response makes sense and for spelling and grammar errors.*

16. For an hour afterwards they seemed undecided; but in the end they bound him to a tree, and were preparing to kill him with their arrows.

17. But a deeper impression had been made on the mind of their chief, who, holding up the compass in his hand, gave the signal to let him go, and Smith, though still guarded as a prisoner, was led to a house, where he was kindly treated and entertained.

18. The Chief Indian asked Powhatan, the king or prince of the country, what they should do with Smith. The Prince met Smith with much celebration, but soon after ordered him to be beaten to death.

19. At the place for his execution, Smith was again rescued, but this time by Pocahontas, the favourite daughter of the chief. She thought this was the wrong decision for her people. She threw her arms round the prisoner, and said, she would save him or die with him.

20. Her kindness won over the cruelty of her tribe, and the king not only gave Smith his life, but soon after sent him back to Jamestown, where Pocahontas continued to follow him with supplies of food and goods that saved the colony from starvation.

21. Captain Smith continued for some time to govern the colony with great wisdom. Soon after he received a dangerous wound from the accidental explosion of some gunpowder. Completely disabled by this, he had to leave his job as captain and return to England. He never returned to the New World again.

Exercises

1. What is the main reason Commander Newport went to the New World?

  E. To take goods and supplies To start a new English colony
  F. To start a war with the natives
  G. To make peace with the natives

2. Which sentence best describes how Newport and his men wound up in what is now called Jamestown?

  A. Landing at Powhatan (Jamestown) was their goal from the start
  B. They were forced to stop there because of threats from the natives
  C. They had to stop there for supplies and stayed because it was good land to start a colony
  D. They had to stop there because of a storm and found the land to be good so they stayed

Re-read paragraph 13.

3. What was the affect of Captain Smith going to get more supplies?

  A. His men had more food to eat
  B. He got captured by some of the natives
  C. He was a hero in his colony
  D. He was killed by the natives

Re-read this phrase from paragraph 21: "Her kindness won over the cruelty of her tribe"

4. What does this phrase most likely mean in the paragraph?

  A. Pocahontas won the war for the colonists
  B. Pocahontas convinced her people not to kill Captain Smith
  C. Pocahontas was so kind that everyone in her tribe was nice to the natives
  D. Pocahontas became the leader of her tribe

5. The Chief Indian does not kill Captain Smith. Why doesn't he kill him? Give 2 reasons why he doesn't kill him. In your answer be sure to include details from the text.

6. Captain Newport's journey to the new world was far from perfect. What went wrong? Name 2 things that went wrong and explain in detail each event. In your answer be sure to include details from the text.

WEEK 8

VIDEO
EXPLANATIONS

ARGOPREP.COM

Daniel's Indian Friend

1. Daniel Boone was a boy who lived on the edge of the deep woods in Pennsylvania. At that time this country still belonged to England.
2. Friendly Indians often came out of the woods to visit the white men. Daniel liked the Indians. He liked them so well that he wished he could live with them.
3. One day he was taking care of his father's cattle. The pasture was several miles from the settlement. Although Daniel was a ten-year-old boy, he sometimes became lonely by himself.
4. Today he lay on a hillside and sang aloud. He wanted to hear a voice, even if it was only his own.
5. There was a low laugh behind him. Daniel sprang to his feet. A tall, slim Indian boy stood a few feet away. The white boy liked him at once.
6. "I sing, too," the young Indian said.
7. He threw back his head and sang. Daniel could not understand a word.
8. "I sing to the sun and the wind and the rain," the boy explained.
9. "I like your Indian song," Daniel said, "but I'm glad you speak English."
10. The boy patted the bow that hung over his right shoulder. "You like this?"
11. The bow was strong and shining. Daniel ran a finger along the smooth wood.
12. "I like it very much," he said.
13. The other boy took an arrow and placed it on the bowstring. He pulled back the bow. The arrow flew away.
14. "You get," the Indian said.
15. Daniel ran after the arrow. He picked it up and looked back. The Indian boy was right beside him.
16. He took the arrow from Daniel. Again he shot it. Again the white boy ran after it. The young Indian ran beside him.
17. He shook his head when Daniel handed him the arrow.
18. He handed Daniel the bow.
19. "Shoot!" he said.
20. Daniel took the bow in his hands. He pulled it back and let the arrow fly.
21. By now Daniel had forgotten the cattle. He had forgotten everything but the wonderful bow, his new friend, and the wide, wild woods.
22. After a while the boys came to a high hill. At the bottom was an Indian village. The brown skinned boy took Daniel by the hand and ran toward the settlement.
23. Several dogs barked at them. Some women were hoeing their gardens. They hardly looked up as the boys passed.
24. An old woman was stirring something in an iron pot over a fire. It smelled good. Daniel remembered that he had eaten nothing since breakfast.
25. His friend stopped and pointed to Daniel and himself. The old woman nodded. With a sharp stick, she lifted a piece of meat from the pot.
26. The Indian boy took a broad leaf from a nearby bush. The woman dropped the hot meat on it.
27. Now Daniel knew what to do. He, too, found a leaf. The woman gave him some meat. Soon the hungry boys had finished their lunch.

What kind of people are the main characters? Use evidence to back up your claim. Understanding the characters better can help you better understand the story as a whole.

28.   That afternoon they swam in the clear, broad river. Then they lay on the bank in the sunshine. Daniel had never been so happy. However, he knew he must soon go home. His mother would worry if he did not return before dark.

29.   "I must go now. I must drive the cows home," he told his Indian friend.

30.   The boy frowned. "Women's work," he told Daniel.

31.   Daniel laughed. "It may be for the Indians, but it's not at the Boones' house. I think I'd like being an Indian. An Indian boy has more fun than a white boy."

32.   "There is much for an Indian to learn," the other told him. "We must learn to hunt, track animals, fish, and find our way in the wilderness."

33.   "Those things are not work. They are fun," Daniel told him. "I wish I were an Indian. I believe I'd make a better Indian than a white boy."

34.   When Daniel reached home at last, his mother scolded him.

35.   "You should not have gone off with that Indian boy. You can't trust the Indians," she told her son.

36.   "He was a good boy. I liked him," Daniel said.

37.   His mother shook her head. "Indians are not like us. We think differently from them."

38.   Daniel said nothing. But he thought his mother was mistaken.

39.   "I believe I can think like an Indian," he said to himself. "Except for color, I'm more like an Indian than a white boy."

Exercises

1. Which best describes how Daniel met the young Indian?

   A. He got lost in the woods and found the young Indian boy singing
   B. He was taking a break from working when a young Indian boy heard him singing
   C. He was working in the woods and came across the young Indian boy who was singing
   D. He had always known of the young Indian boy but his mother told him not to play with Indian boys, but today he didn't care

2. What does Daniel do when he sees the bow?

   A. He tries it shoot it right away
   B. He chases after the arrow the Indian boy shot
   C. He runs away from the bow
   D. He thinks about whether he should shoot the bow or not

Re-read lines 26 through 28.

3. What does Daniel learn by watching the Indian boy?

   A. How to beg for food
   B. How to trick a woman into giving you food
   C. What to do if you are scared by an older person
   D. How to let an Indian woman know you are hungry and how to get the food

4. Which statement best shows how Daniel feels about an Indian's work?

   A. It is hard work
   B. It is a woman's work
   C. It is more fun than work
   D. It's the same work as he has to do

At the end of the story Daniel says: "Except for color, I'm more like an Indian than a white boy."

5. Which statement best describes Daniel's feelings?

   A. He didn't like the Indians before, but now he realizes he is just like them
   B. He doesn't like the way his father and mother act so he sees himself more like an Indian
   C. He wishes he had the work that Indians do and realizes he thinks more like an Indian than a white boy
   D. He doesn't like the fact that he is more like an Indian than a white boy

Re-read lines 36-38.

6. What do we learn about Daniel's mother in these lines?

   A. She doesn't trust the Indians and doesn't want Daniel to play with them
   B. She didn't trust the Indians before but now that Daniel has met a friend she likes them
   C. She's afraid of Indians because in the past they have hurt her
   D. She thinks the Indians think the same way as she does

Notes

1. Saving The Birds

2. One day in spring four men were riding on horseback along a country road. These men were lawyers, and they were going to the next town to attend court.

3. There had been a rain, and the ground was very soft. Water was dripping from the trees, and the grass was wet.

4. The four lawyers rode along, one behind another; for the pathway was narrow, and the mud on each side of it was deep. They rode slowly, and talked and laughed and were very jolly.

5. As they were passing through a grove of small trees, they heard a great fluttering over their heads and a feeble chirping in the grass by the roadside.

6. "Stith! stith! stith!" came from the leafy branches above them.

7. "Cheep! cheep! cheep!" came from the wet grass.

8. "What is the matter here?" asked the first lawyer, whose name was Speed. "Oh, it's only some old robins!" said the second lawyer, whose name was Hardin. "The storm has blown two of the little ones out of the nest. They are too young to fly, and the mother bird is making a great fuss about it."

9. "What a pity! They'll die down there in the grass," said the third lawyer, whose name I forget.

10. "Oh, well! They're nothing but birds," said Mr. Hardin. "Why should we bother?"

11. "Yes, why should we?" said Mr. Speed.

12. The three men, as they passed, looked down and saw the little birds fluttering in the cold, wet grass. They saw the mother robin flying about, and crying to her mate.

13. Then they rode on, talking and laughing as before. In a few minutes they had forgotten about the birds.

14. But the fourth lawyer, whose name was Abraham Lincoln, stopped. He got down from his horse and very gently took the little ones up in his big warm hands.

15. They did not seem frightened, but chirped softly, as if they knew they were safe.

16. "Never mind, my little fellows," said Mr. Lincoln "I will put you in your own cozy little bed."

17. Then he looked up to find the nest from which they had fallen. It was high, much higher than he could reach.

18. But Mr. Lincoln could climb. He had climbed many a tree when he was a boy. He put the birds softly, one by one, into their warm little home. Two other baby birds were there, that had not fallen out. All cuddled down together and were very happy.

19. Soon the three lawyers who had ridden ahead stopped at a spring to give their horses water.

20. "Where is Lincoln?" asked one.

21. All were surprised to find that he was not with them.

22. "Do you remember those birds?" said Mr. Speed. "Very likely he has stopped to take care of them."

23. In a few minutes Mr. Lincoln joined them. His shoes were covered with mud; he had torn his coat on the thorny tree.

24. "Hello, Abraham!" said Mr. Hardin. "Where have you been?"

25. "I stopped a minute to give those birds to their mother," he answered.

26. "Well, we always thought you were a hero," said Mr. Speed. "Now we know it."

27. Then all three of them laughed heartily. They thought it so foolish that a strong man should take so much trouble just for some worthless young birds.

Stop and think every few paragraphs or lines and think, "Do I understand what I just read?" If not, go back and re-read. If you do, think about jotting down some notes.

28. "Gentlemen," said Mr. Lincoln, "I could not have slept to-night, if I had left those helpless little robins to perish in the wet grass."

29. Abraham Lincoln afterwards became very famous as a lawyer and statesman. He was elected president. Next to Washington he was the greatest American.

Exercises

1. What does the word narrow mean as it is used in paragraph 4?

  A. Not very good
  B. Thin
  C. Wide
  D. Gross

4. Which is the best theme for this story?

  A. Your friends should always be loyal to you
  B. Don't be greedy
  C. Work hard
  D. Help out those who might need help

Re-read lines 14-16.

2. What do we learn about Abraham Lincoln in these lines?

  A. He was not a lawyer
  B. He cares about animals and birds
  C. He thinks his lawyer friends are mean
  D. He needs to get to work fast

Re-read line 23.

5. Why do you think the author included this information in the passage?

  A. To show that Lincoln was a messy dresser
  B. To show that he was poor and couldn't afford more clothes
  C. To show that he had gotten down and dirty to help the little birds
  D. So that his friends can make fun of him

3. How would you describe the relationship between Lincoln and the other lawyers?

  A. Lincoln likes the other lawyers, but thinks they should be more caring about the little things
  B. Lincoln hates the other lawyers because they did not stop to help the birds
  C. The other lawyers think Lincoln is a fool and hate him
  D. The other lawyers think Lincoln is a hero and look up to him

Re-read lines 26 and 27.

6. Which best describes what the other 3 lawyers were saying about Lincoln?

  A. He is a hero, a kind and brave man, so they celebrated him
  B. He is a smart man for stopping to save the birds
  C. He is foolish, because he is so strong and smart. He should have bigger things to deal with than birds so they made fun of him
  D. He is an animal lover

Saved by a Dolphin

1. In the city of Corinth there once lived a wonderful musician whose name was Arion. No other person could play on the lyre or sing so sweetly as he; and the songs which he composed were famous in many lands.

2. The king of Corinth was his friend. The people of Corinth never grew tired of praising his sweet music.

3. One summer he went over the sea to Italy; for his name was well known there, and many people wished to hear him sing.

4. He visited several cities, and in each place he was well paid for his music.

5. At last, having become quite rich, he decided to go home. There was a ship just ready to sail for Corinth, and the captain agreed to take him as a passenger.

6. The sea was rough. The ship was driven far out of her course. Many days passed before they came in sight of land.

7. The sailors were rude and unruly. The captain himself had been a robber.

8. When they heard that Arion had a large sum of money with him they began to make plans to get it.

9. "The easiest way," said the captain, "is to throw him overboard. Then there will be no one to tell tales."

10. Arion overheard them plotting.

11. "You may take everything that I have," he said, "if you will only spare my life."

12. But they had made up their minds to get rid of him. They feared that if they were to spare him he should report the matter to the king.

13. "Your life we will not spare," they said; "but we will give you the choice of two things. You must either jump overboard into the sea or be slain with your own sword. Which shall it be?"

14. "I shall jump overboard," said Arion, "but I pray that you will first grant me a favor."

15. "What is it?" asked the captain.

16. "Allow me to sing to you my latest and best song. I promise that as soon as it is finished I will leap into the sea."

17. The sailors agreed; for they wanted to hear the musician whose songs were famous all over the world.

18. Arion dressed himself in his finest clothing. He took his stand on the forward deck, while the robber sailors stood in a half circle before him, waiting to listen to his song.

19. He touched his lyre and began to play his song. Then he sang a wonderful song, so sweet, so lively, so touching, that many of the sailors were moved to tears.

20. And now they would have spared him; but he was true to his promise,— as soon as the song was finished, he threw himself headfirst into the sea.

21. The sailors divided his money among themselves; and the ship sailed on. In a short time they reached Corinth in safety, and the king sent an officer to bring the captain and his men to the palace.

22. "Are you lately from Italy?" he asked.

23. "We are," they answered.

24. "What news can you give me concerning my friend Arion, the sweetest of all musicians?"

25. "He was well and happy when we left Italy," they answered. "He has a mind to spend the rest of his life in that country."

Don't just underline information you think may be important. Underline evidence to answer questions or evidence to back up your ideas about characters.

26. Just as they had spoken these words the door opened and Arion himself stood before them. He was dressed just as they had seen him when he jumped into the sea. They were so astonished that they fell upon their knees before the king and told the truth.
27. Now, how was Arion saved from drowning when he leaped overboard?
28. Old story-tellers say that he fell on the back of a large fish, called a dolphin, which had been charmed by his music and was swimming near the ship. The dolphin carried him with great speed to the nearest shore. Then, full of joy, the musician hurried to Corinth, not stopping even to change his dress.
29. He told his wonderful story to the king; but the king would not believe him.
30. "Wait," said he, "till the ship arrives, and then we shall know the truth." Three hours later, the ship came into port, as you have already learned. Other people think that the dolphin which saved Arion was not a fish, but a ship named the Dolphin. They say that Arion, being a good swimmer, kept himself afloat until this ship happened to pass by and rescued him from the waves.

Exercises

1. Why does Arion go to Italy?

   A. To visit a family member
   B. To go on vacation
   C. To play concerts for his fans
   D. To make friends

3. Which statement shows why the captain and sailors couldn't spare Arion's life?

   A. They wanted the money for themselves
   B. They would be rewarded
   C. They didn't want to get caught for stealing from him
   D. They thought he was a bad man

Read this phrase from line 11: "if you will only spare my life."

2. What do you think it means in this passage?

   A. Don't kill me
   B. Don't hurt me
   C. Don't steal from me
   D. Take all the money you want

Re-read this sentence from paragraph 26: "They were so astonished that they fell upon their knees before the king and told the truth."

4. What do you think the word astonished means?

   A. Angry
   B. Sad
   C. Happy
   D. Surprised

5. In the story "Saved by a Dolphin" the sailors and the captain of the ship try to kill Arion. How does he survive? What decisions or actions did Arion make that helped save himself? Give 2 examples. Use details from the text to support your answer.

6. In the story "Saved by a Dolphin" there are 2 versions of how Arion survived. Explain each version in your own words. Use details from the text to support your answer.

WEEK 9

VIDEO
EXPLANATIONS

ARGOPREP.COM

The Paddle-Wheel Boat

1. More than a hundred years ago, two boys were fishing in a small river. They sat in a heavy flat bottomed boat, each holding a long, crooked rod in his hands and eagerly waiting for "a bite."

2. When they wanted to move the boat from one place to another they had to pole it; that is, they pushed against a long pole, the lower end of which reached the bottom of the stream.

3. "This is slow work, Robert," said the older of the boys as they were poling up the river to a new fishing place. "The old boat creeps over the water no faster than a snail."

4. "Yes, Christopher; and it is hard work, too," answered Robert. "I think there ought to be some better way of moving a boat."

5. "Yes, there is a better way, and that is by rowing," said Christopher.

6. "But we have no oars."

7. "Well, I can make some oars," said Robert; "but I think there ought to be still another and a better way. I am going to find such a way if I can."

8. The next day Robert's aunt heard a great pounding and sawing in her woodshed. The two boys were there, busily working with hammer and saw.

9. "What are you making, Robert?" she asked.

10. "Oh, I have a plan for making a boat move without poling it or rowing it," he answered.

11. His aunt laughed and said, "Well, I hope that you will succeed."

12. After a great deal of tinkering and trying, they did succeed in making two paddle wheels. They were very rough and crude, but strong and serviceable. They fastened each of these wheels to the end of an iron rod which they passed through the boat from side to side. The rod was bent in the middle so that it could be turned as with a crank. When the work was finished, the old fishing boat looked rather odd, with a paddle wheel on each side which dipped just a few inches into the water. The boys lost no time in trying it.

13. "She goes ahead all right," said Christopher, "but how shall we guide her?"

14. "Oh, I have thought of that," said Robert. He took something like an oarlock from his pocket and fastened it to the back of the boat; then with a paddle which worked with this oarlock one of the boys could guide the boat while the other turned the paddle wheels.

15. "It is better than poling the boat," said Christopher.

16. "It is better than rowing, too," said Robert. "See how fast she goes!"

17. That night when Christopher went home he had a wonderful story to tell. "Robert Fulton planned the whole thing," he said, "and I helped him make the paddles and put them on the boat."

18. "I wonder why we didn't think of something like that long ago," said his father. "Almost anybody could rig up an old boat like that."

19. "Yes, I wonder, too," said Christopher. "It looks easy enough, now that Robert has shown how it is done."

20. When Robert Fulton became a man, he did not forget his experiment with the old fishing boat. He kept on, planning and thinking and working, until at last he succeeded in making a boat with paddle wheels that could be run by steam.

21. He is now remembered and honored as the inventor of the steam boat. He became famous because he was always thinking and studying and working.

TIP of the **DAY**

Answer choices that don't sound grammatically correct usually aren't. Don't waste time trying to figure out what the answer choice means, it's probably not correct.

Exercises

Re-read paragraphs 2 and 3.

1. Why did the author most likely include this information?

    A. To show how people caught fish
    B. To teach others how to "pole" in a boat
    C. To explain that this method of moving the boat was not very good
    D. To show that the boys were hard workers

Read this sentence from paragraph 12: "They were very rough and crude, but strong and serviceable."

2. Which best describes what the author was trying to say about the paddle wheel?

    A. They weren't perfect looking but they worked well
    B. They were great looking but didn't work as well as they had hoped
    C. They were rough to the touch and barely worked
    D. They worked, but didn't last very long

3. Which best describes how the boys get the paddle wheels to move?

    A. With a steam engine attached to the back of the boat
    B. The oarlock helps the paddles to move
    C. They turned a crank to move the paddles
    D. They use poles to move the paddles along the river

Re-read paragraph 14.

4. What is an oarlock?

    A. A paddle that locks into place
    B. Something that holds the paddle into place to help steer
    C. A lock for the boat so no one can steal the oars
    D. A special paddle for this new invention

5. Which best describes how Christopher's parents felt about Robert, and his invention of the paddle wheel?

    A. They thought he was lucky because it was an easy invention, and he was just the first to think of it
    B. They thought he was clever and wise for coming up with an idea that no one had thought of
    C. They thought he was a genius for creating such a complicated and detailed invention
    D. They thought he was rude for bragging about his invention

6. Which best describes how the author chose to organize this passage?

    A. Describe how the paddle wheel works, show the need for it, coming up with the idea
    B. Describe how the paddle wheel works, coming up with the idea, show the need for it
    C. Show the need for it, describe how the paddle wheel works, coming up with the idea
    D. Show the need for it, coming up with the idea, describe how the paddle wheel works

Why He Carried the Turkey

1. In Richmond, Virginia, one Saturday morning, an old man went into the market to buy something. He was dressed plainly, his coat was worn, and his hat was dingy. On his arm he carried a small basket.

2. "I wish to get a fowl for to-morrow's dinner," he said.

3. The market man showed him a fat turkey, plump and white and ready for roasting.

4. "Ah! that is just what I want," said the old man. "My wife will be delighted with it."

5. He asked the price and paid for it. The market man wrapped a paper round it and put it in the basket.

6. Just then a young man stepped up. "I will take one of those turkeys," he said. He was dressed in fine style and carried a small cane.

7. "Shall I wrap it up for you?" asked the market man.

8. "Yes, here is your money," answered the young gentleman; "and send it to my house at once."

9. "I cannot do that," said the market man. "My errand boy is sick to-day, and there is no one else to send. Besides, it is not our custom to deliver goods."

10. "Then how am I to get it home?" asked the young gentleman.

11. "I suppose you will have to carry it yourself," said the market man. "It is not heavy."

12. "Carry it myself! Who do you think I am? Fancy me carrying a turkey along the street!" said the young gentleman; and he began to grow very angry. The old man who had bought the first turkey was standing quite near. He had heard all that was said.

13. "Excuse me, sir," he said; "but may I ask where you live?"

14. "I live at Number 39, Blank Street," answered the young gentleman; "and my name is Johnson."

15. "Well, that is lucky," said the old man, smiling. "I happen to be going that way, and I will carry your turkey, if you will allow me."

16. "Oh, certainly!" said Mr. Johnson. "Here it is. You may follow me."

17. When they reached Mr. Johnson's house, the old man politely handed him the turkey and turned to go.

18. "Here, my friend, what shall I pay you?" said the young gentleman.

19. "Oh, nothing, sir, nothing," answered the old man. "It was no trouble to me, and you are welcome."

20. He bowed and went on. Young Mr. Johnson looked after him and wondered. Then he turned and walked briskly back to the market.

21. "Who is that polite old gentleman who carried my turkey for me?" he asked of the market man.

22. "That is John Marshall, Chief Justice of the United States. He is one of the greatest men in our country," was the answer.

23. The young gentleman was surprised and ashamed. "Why did he offer to carry my turkey?" he asked.

24. "He wished to teach you a lesson," answered the market man.

25. "What sort of lesson?" "He wished to teach you that no man should feel himself too fine to carry his own packages."

26. "Oh, no!" said another man who had seen and heard it all. "Judge Marshall carried the turkey simply because he wished to be kind. That is his way."

  *If a question (like number 2) refers to a paragraph go back and re-read that paragraph. Use evidence only from that paragraph to help you reach your answer.*

Exercises

1. Which sentence from the passage best helps you understand what a "fowl" is?

   A. "I wish to get a fowl for to-morrow's dinner," he said.
   B. The market man showed him a fat turkey, plump and white and ready for roasting.
   C. "Ah! that is just what I want," said the old man. "My wife will be delighted with it."
   D. "Shall I wrap it up for you?" asked the market man.

2. What do we learn about the young boy in paragraph 12?

   A. He is a young prince
   B. He thinks he is too important to carry the turkey himself
   C. He needs help carrying the turkey because he isn't strong enough
   D. He wanted to pay someone to carry the turkey for him

Re-read paragraph 25.

3. Which is most likely the reason the market man told the young boy that Judge Marshall wanted to teach him a lesson?

   A. The young boy was rude to the market man, who thought he needed to be taught a lesson
   B. He knew Judge Marshall well and thought this was why he carried the turkey
   C. He made his best guess at Judge Marshall's reason for carrying the turkey
   D. He was upset with Judge Marshall for carrying the turkey

4. Which best describes a difference between the young boy and Judge Marshall?

   A. The young boy was dressed in dirty old clothes but acted important and Judge Marshall was dressed nicely and acted kind
   B. The young boy was dressed in dirty old clothes and acted needy and Judge Marshall was dressed nicely and acted important
   C. Judge Marshall was dressed in dirty old clothes and acted kindly but the boy was dressed nicely and acted important
   D. Judge Marshall and the boy were both dressed nicely, but the boy acted important the Judge Marshall acted kindly

5. What best describes the main theme in this passage?

   A. Always be kind to strangers
   B. Don't trust that a man in old clothes is unimportant
   C. Act kind to everyone and don't think you're too important to do anything
   D. Give to charity and do favors for others

6. What is most likely the reason Judge Marshall was wearing dirty and old clothes?

   A. He was too poor to afford new clothes
   B. He liked the way the old clothes looked and felt
   C. He didn't want other people to know how important he was, he wanted to be treated normally
   D. He didn't like the attention of being a famous Judge

The Ice Age

1. The struggle to keep alive during the cold period was terrible. Many races of men and animals, whose bones we have found, disappeared from the face of the earth. Whole tribes and clans were wiped out by hunger and cold and want.
2. This part of my history is very difficult because the changes which I must describe were so very slow and so very gradual.
3. Nature is never in a hurry. She has all eternity in which to accomplish her task and she can afford to bring about the necessary changes with deliberate care.
4. Prehistoric man lived through at least four definite eras when the ice descended far down into the valleys and covered the greater part of the European continent.
5. The last one of these periods came to an end almost thirty thousand years ago.
6. From that moment on man left behind him concrete evidence of his existence in the form of tools and arms and pictures and in a general way we can say that history begins when the last cold period had become a thing of the past.
7. The endless struggle for life had taught the survivors many things.
8. Stone and wooden tools had become as common as steel tools are in our own days.
9. Gradually the poorly chipped flint axe had been replaced by one of polished flint which was way more practical. It allowed man to attack many animals, which they could not have attacked because of their size and strength.
10. The mammoth was no longer seen.
11. The musk-ox had retreated to the polar circle.
12. The tiger had left Europe for good.
13. The cave-bear no longer ate little children.
14. The powerful brain of the weakest and most helpless of all living creatures--Man--had devised such strong instruments of destruction that he was now the master of all the other animals.
15. The first great victory over Nature had been gained but many others were to follow.
16. Equipped with a full set of tools both for hunting and fishing, the cave-dweller looked for new living quarters.
17. The shores of rivers and lakes offered the best opportunity for a regular livelihood.
18. The old caves were deserted and the human race moved toward the water.
19. Now that man could handle heavy axes, the cutting of trees no longer offered any great difficulties.
20. For countless ages birds had been constructing comfortable houses out of chips of wood and grass amidst the branches of trees.
21. Man followed their example.
22. He, too, built himself a nest and called it his "home."
23. He did not, except in a few parts of Asia, take to the trees which were a bit too small and unsteady for his purpose.
24. He cut down a number of logs. These he drove firmly into the soft bottom of a shallow lake. On top of them he constructed a wooden platform and upon this platform he erected his first wooden house.
25. It offered many advantages over the old cave.
26. No wild animals could break into it and robbers could not enter it. The lake itself was an endless store room containing an endless supply of fresh fish.

When answering questions about unknown words or phrases plug each answer choice into the text to see which makes the most sense.

27. These houses built on piles were much healthier than the old caves and they gave the children a chance to grow up into strong men. The population increased steadily and man began to occupy vast spaces of wilderness which had been unused since the beginning of time.
28. And all the time new inventions were made which made life more comfortable and less dangerous.
29. Often enough these innovations were not due to the cleverness of man's brain. He simply copied the animals.
30. You know of course that there are a large number of beasts who prepare for the long winter by burying nuts and a corns and other food which is abundant during the summer. Just think of the squirrels who are forever filling their larder in gardens and parks with supplies for the winter and the early spring.
31. Early man, less intelligent in many respects than the squirrels, had not known how to save anything for the future.
32. He ate until his hunger was gone, but what he did not need right away he allowed to rot. As a result he often went without his meals during the cold period and many of his family died from hunger.
33. Until he followed the example of the animals and prepared for the future by saving when the harvest had been good and there was an abundance of wheat and grain.
34. He had managed to survive the ice and the snow and the wild animals and that in itself, was a great deal.

Exercises

Re-read paragraphs 9-13.

1. What caused all of these animals to disappear?

  A. The ice age
  B. Lack of food
  C. Better land in other places
  D. Man had killed them and scared them away

3. Which best describes why man built his first home in a lake?

  A. So they could swim and have fun
  B. The water would hold up the house stronger
  C. They had so many fish to eat right by their home
  D. They no longer wanted to live on the land

Re-read paragraph 3.

2. What do you think the author meant by deliberate care in this sentence?

  A. Caring a little bit
  B. Doing it on purpose in her own time with care
  C. Doing it without care
  D. Rushing to get it done

Re-read the last paragraph in the passage.

4. Why does the author conclude the passage in this way?

  A. To show that he thought man was pretty stupid and surviving the ice age was surprising
  B. To show that in the toughest of times man was pretty wise to invent things in order to survive and that was impressive
  C. To explain that surviving was easy and anyone should have been able to do this
  D. To explain how man survived

5. In the passage man learns some tricks and lessons from animals. What does he learn? Give 2 examples of things he has learned by watching the animals. Be sure to include details from the text to support your answer.

_____

_____

_____

_____

_____

_____

_____

_____

6. In this passage man changed how they lived quite a bit. What are some things man changed in order to survive? Give 2 examples. Be sure to include details from the text to support your answer.

_____

_____

_____

_____

_____

_____

_____

_____

WEEK 10

VIDEO
EXPLANATIONS

ARGOPREP.COM

The Midnight Ride

1. The midnight ride of Paul Revere happened a long time ago when this country was ruled by the king of England.

2. There were thousands of English soldiers in Boston. The king had sent them there to make the people obey his unjust laws. These soldiers guarded the streets of the town; they would not let anyone go out or come in without their permission.

3. The people did not like this. They said, "We have a right to be free men, but the king treats us as slaves. He makes us pay taxes and gives us nothing in return. He sends soldiers among us to take away our liberty."

4. The whole country was stirred up. Brave men left their homes and hurried toward Boston.

5. They said, "We do not wish to fight against the king, but we are free men, and he must not send soldiers to oppress us. If the people of Boston must fight for their liberty, we will help them." These men were not afraid of the king's soldiers. Some of them camped in Charlestown, a village near Boston. From the hills of Charlestown they could watch and see what the king's soldiers were doing.

6. They wished to be ready to defend themselves, if the soldiers should try to do them harm. For this reason they had bought some gun powder and stored it at Concord, nearly twenty miles away.

7. When the king's soldiers heard about this powder, they made up their minds to go out and get it for themselves.

8. Among the watchers at Charlestown was a brave young man named Paul Revere. He was ready to serve his country in any way that he could. One day a friend of his who lived in Boston came to see him. He came very quietly and secretly, to escape the soldiers.

9. "I have something to tell you," he said. "Some of the king's soldiers are going to Concord to get the powder that is there. They are getting ready to start this very night."

10. "Indeed!" said Paul Revere. "They shall get no powder, if I can help it. I will stir up all the farmers between here and Concord, and those fellows will have a hot time of it. But you must help me."

11. "I will do all that I can," said his friend.

12. "Well, then," said Paul Revere, "you must go back to Boston and watch. Watch, and as soon as the soldiers are ready to start, hang a lantern in the tower of the old North Church. If they are to cross the river, hang two. I will be here, ready. As soon as I see the light, I will mount my horse and ride out to give the alarm."

13. And so it was done. When night came, Paul Revere was at the river side with his horse. He looked over toward Boston. He knew where the old North Church stood, but he could not see much in the darkness.

14. Hour after hour he stood and watched. The town seemed very still; but now and then he could hear the beating of a drum or the shouting of some soldier.

15. The moon rose, and by its light he could see the dim form of the church tower, far away. He heard the clock strike ten. He waited and watched. The clock struck eleven. He was beginning to feel tired. Perhaps the soldiers had given up their plan.

16. He walked up and down the river bank, leading his horse behind him; but he kept his eyes turned always toward the dim, dark spot which he knew was the old North Church.

When answering questions about unknown words or phrases plug each answer choice into the text to see which makes the most sense.

17. All at once a light flashed out from the tower. "Ah! there it is!" he cried. The soldiers had started. He spoke to his horse. He put his foot in the stirrup. He was ready to mount.

18. Then another light flashed clear and bright by the side of the first one. The soldiers would cross the river.

19. Paul Revere sprang into the saddle. Like a bird let loose, his horse leaped forward. Away they went. Away they went through the village street and out upon the country road. "Up! up!" shouted Paul Revere. "The soldiers are coming! Up! up! And defend yourselves!"

20. The cry awoke the farmers; they sprang from their beds and looked out. They could not see the speeding horse, but they heard the clatter of its hoofs far down the road, and they understood the cry, "Up! up! and defend yourselves!"

21. "It is the alarm! The red coats are coming," they said to each other. Then they took their guns, their axes, anything they could find, and hurried out.

22. So, through the night, Paul Revere rode toward Concord. At every farmhouse and every village he repeated his call. The alarm quickly spread. Guns were fired. Bells were rung. The people for miles around were roused as though a fire were raging.

23. The king's soldiers were surprised to find everybody awake along the road. They were angry because their plans had been discovered. When they reached Concord, they burned the courthouse there.

24. At Lexington, not far from Concord, there was a sharp fight in which several men were killed. This, in history, is called the Battle of Lexington. It was the beginning of the war called the Revolutionary War. But the king's soldiers did not find the gunpowder. They were glad enough to march back without it. All along the road the farmers were waiting for them. It seemed as if every man in the country was after them. And they did not feel themselves safe until they were once more in Boston.

Exercises

Re-read the sentence from paragraph 4. "The whole country was stirred up."

1. What do you think the author was trying to tell you in this sentence?

   A. The people in the country were confused
   B. The people in the country were very angry
   C. The country did not know where to look for help
   D. The country was a mix of all different kinds of people

4. How does Paul feel while waiting for the the lantern to be lit in the church?

   A. Scared
   B. Anxious
   C. Happy
   D. Angry

2. Which statement best describes the reason the people bought gunpowder?

   A. They wanted to go to war against the king
   B. They wanted to have the gunpowder to sell to the soldiers
   C. They needed the gun powder to fight off soldiers that were already attacking
   D. They wanted to have the gunpowder to be ready in case the soldiers attacked

5. Which detail best shows how Paul helped the people?

   A. When night came, Paul Revere was at the riverside with his horse.
   B. Paul Revere sprang into the saddle.
   C. "Ah! there it is!" he cried.
   D. "Up! up!" shouted Paul Revere. "The soldiers are coming! Up! up! And defend yourselves!"

Re-read paragraph 12.

3. Which statement is true about how Paul Revere's friend warned him that the British were coming to steal the gunpowder?

   A. He rung the bell in the church tower to warn Paul Revere
   B. He lit 2 lanterns to signal that the British were ready to start
   C. He crossed the river on a horse to tell Paul the British were coming
   D. He lit 1 lantern to signal that the British were ready to start

6. Which sentence describes Paul Revere?

   A. He was scared of the British so warned people
   B. He wanted the people to be able to defend themselves against the British so he warned them
   C. He was a General in the army and it was his duty to warn the people about the British
   D. He was angry that the British were taking over so he planned an attack against them

Notes

An excerpt from **Little Women**

1. "Christmas won't be Christmas without any presents," grumbled Jo, lying on the rug

2. "It's so dreadful to be poor!" sighed Meg, looking down at her old dress.

3. "I don't think it's fair for some girls to have plenty of pretty things, and other girls nothing at all," added little Amy, with an injured sniff.

4. "We've got Father and Mother, and each other," said Beth contentedly from her corner.

5. The four young faces on which the firelight shone brightened at the cheerful words, but darkened again as Jo said sadly, "We haven't got Father, and shall not have him for along time." She didn't say "perhaps never," but each silently added it, thinking of Father far away, where the fighting was.

6. Nobody spoke for a minute; then Meg said in an saddened tone, "You know the reason Mother suggested not having any presents this Christmas was because it is going to be a hard winter for everyone; and she thinks we ought not to spend money for fun, when our men are suffering so in the army. We can't do much, but we can make our littlesacrifices, and ought to do it gladly. But I am afraid I don't," and Meg shook her head, as she thought regretfully of all the pretty things she wanted.

7. "But I don't think the little we should spend would do any good. We've each got a dollar, and the army wouldn't be much helped by our giving that. I agree not to expect anything from Mother or you, but I do want to buy Undine and Sintran for myself. I've wanted it so long," said Jo, who was a bookworm.

8. "I planned to spend mine in new music," said Beth, with a little sigh, which no one heard.

9. "I shall get a nice box of Faber's drawing pencils; I really need them," said Amy decidedly.

10. "Mother didn't say anything about our money, and she won't wish us to give up everything. Let's each buy what we want, and have a little fun; I'm sure we've worked hard enough to earn it," cried Jo.

11. "I know I do—teaching those tiresome children nearly all day, when I'm longing to enjoy myself at home," began Meg, in the complaining tone again.

12. "You don't have half such a hard time as I do," said Jo. "How would you like to be shut up for hours with a nervous, fussy old lady, who keeps you trotting, is never satisfied, and worries you till you're ready to fly out the window or cry?"

13. "It's naughty to fret, but I do think washing dishes and keeping things tidy is the worst work in the world. It makes me cross, and my hands get so stiff, I can't practice well at all." And Beth looked at her rough hands with a sigh that anyone could hear that time.

14. "I don't believe any of you suffer as I do," cried Amy, "for you don't have to go to school with impertinent girls, who plague you if you don't know your lessons, and laugh at your dresses, and label your father if he isn't rich, and insult you when your nose isn't nice."

15. "Don't peck at one another, children. Don't you wish we had the money Papa lost when we were little, Jo? Dear me! How happy and good we'd be, if we had no worries!" said Meg, who could remember better times.

16. "You said the other day you thought we were a deal happier than the King's children, for they were fighting and fretting all the time, in spite of their money."

17. "So I did, Beth. Well, I think we are. For though we do have to work, we make fun of ourselves, and are a pretty jolly set, as Jo would say."

18. "Jo does use such slang words!" observed Amy, with a look at the long figure stretched on the rug.

Skip hard questions. Most likely questions do not get harder as you move on. You might find some easy questions later on. Take a deep breath.

19. Jo immediately sat up, put her hands in her pockets, and began to whistle.
20. "Don't, Jo. It's so boyish!"
21. "That's why I do it."
22. "I detest rude, unladylike girls!""I hate affected, niminy-piminy chits!"
23. "Birds in their little nests agree," sang Beth, the peacemaker, with such a funny face that both sharp voices softened to a laugh, and the "pecking" ended for that time.

Exercises

1. In paragraph 5 what information do we learn about the girls' father?

   A. He was dead
   B. He was fighting in the war
   C. He was poor
   D. He was not a nice father

2. What does the word detest mean as it is used in paragraph 22?

   A. Love
   B. Hate
   C. Like a little
   D. Dislike a little

3. Which statement is true about the girls and their gifts?

   A. They didn't want their mother spending money on them
   B. They only had $1 and that little money wasn't going to be useful to the army so they spent it on themselves instead of donating it
   C. They had wanted these gifts for so long and decided it was only fair for them to give themselves a gift so they put all their money together and bought gifts
   D. The army needed the money so they decided to donate it

4. Which detail best helps you understand what Undine and Sintran is?

   A. Who was a bookworm
   B. We've each got a dollar
   C. I agree not to expect anything from Mother or you
   D. I planned to spend mine in new music

5. Which statement best describes paragraphs 11-14?

   A. The girls are giving each other credit for working hard
   B. The girls are complaining about how hard they work
   C. The girls are talking about giving each other gifts
   D. The girls are thinking about what to do with the money

6. Which statement would belong in a summary of this story?

   A. 4 young girls want to give their father a gift for christmas
   B. Everybody wants to help the army so the girls save their money
   C. The girls are quite poor, but they use the little money they have to treat themselves to a small gift
   D. The mother is very upset with the girls for arguing about their jobs

Why the Crocodile Has a Wide Mouth

1. "Come to my kingdom whenever you will," said the goddess of the water to the king of the land. "My waves will be calm, and my animals will be gentle. They will be as good to your children as if they were my own. Nothing in all my kingdom will do you harm."

2. The goddess went back to her home in the sea, and the king walked to the shore of the river and stood gazing upon the beautiful water. Beside him walked his youngest son.

3. "Father," asked the boy, "would the goddess be angry if I went into the water to swim?"

4. "No," answered the father. "She says that nothing in all her wide kingdom will do us harm. The water-animals will be kind, and the waves will be calm."

5. The boy went into the water. He could swim as easily as a fish, and he went from shore to shore, sometimes talking with the fishes, sometimes getting a bright piece of stone to carry to his father. Suddenly something caught him by the foot and dragged him down, down, through the deep, dark water. "Oh, father!" he cried, but his father had gone away from the shore, and the strange creature, whatever it was, dragged the boy down to the very bottom of the river.

6. The river was full of sorrow for what the creature had done, and it lifted the boy gently and bore him to the feet of the goddess. His eyes were closed and his face was white, for he was dead. Great tears came from the eyes of the goddess when she looked at him. "I did not think any of my animals would do such a cruel thing," she said. "His father shall never know it, for the boy shall not remember what has happened."

7. Then she laid her warm hand upon his head, and whispered some words of magic into his ear. "Open your eyes," she called, and soon they were wide open. "You went in to swim," said the goddess. "Did the water please you?"

8. "Yes, surely."

9. "Were the water-animals kind to you?"

10. "Yes, surely," answered the boy, for the magic words had kept him from remembering anything about the strange creature that had dragged him to the bottom of the river.

11. The boy went home to his father, and as soon as he was out of sight, the goddess called to the water-animals, "Come one, come all, come little, come great."

12. "It is the voice of the goddess," said the water-animals, and they all began to swim to ward her as fast as they could.

13. When they were together before her, she said, "One of you has been cruel and wicked. One of you has dragged to the bottom of the river the son of my friend, the king of the land, but I have carried him safely to shore, and now he is in his home. When he comes again, will you watch over him wherever in the wide, wide water he may wish to go?"

14. "Yes!" "Yes!" "Yes!" cried the water-animals.

15. "Water," asked the goddess, "will you be calm and still when the son of my friend is my guest?"

16. "Gladly," answered the water.

17. Suddenly the goddess caught sight of the crocodile hiding behind the other animals. "Will you be kind to the boy and keep harm away from him?" she asked.

  TIP of the DAY

For short response answers restate the question or first part of the question to help introduce your answer. It will make you sound like an expert.

18.   Now it was the crocodile that had dragged the boy to the bottom of the river. He wished to say, "Yes," but he did not dare to open his mouth fear of saying, "I did it, I did it," so he said not a word. The goddess cried, "Did you drag the king's son to the bottom of the river?" Still the crocodile dared not open his mouth for fear of saying, "I did it, I did it." Then the goddess was angry. She drew her long sword, and saying, "The mouth that will not open when it should must be made to open," she struck the crocodile's mouth with the sword. "Oh, look!" cried the other animals. The crocodile's mouth had opened; there was no question about that, for it had split open so far that he was afraid he should never be able to keep it closed.

Exercises

1. Which best describes how paragraph 5 relates to paragraph 6?

   A. Paragraph 5 shows the boy getting caught in the water and paragraph 6 shows how he was brought back to life
   B. Paragraph 5 shows the boy getting caught in the water and paragraph 6 shows how the goddess felt about what happened and what she would do
   C. Paragraph 5 shows the boy making the decision to go in the water and paragraph 6 shows the boy's final choice
   D. Paragraph 5 explains what will happen in paragraph 6

Re-read this line from paragraph 6, "The river was full of sorry for what the creature had done."

3. What is the author trying to tell you?

   A. The river was happy the creature had been caught
   B. The river was angry at the goddess for letting the boy get dragged to the bottom
   C. The river was sad because the creature dragged the boy to the bottom
   D. The river was full from eating so much

2. Which statement best describes why the goddess of the water wants to keep the boy safe?

   A. She always protects people who go into the water
   B. She made the king of the land a promise to keep the boy safe
   C. She wants to get land for herself so she wants to keep the boy safe
   D. She is the mother of the boy

4. Which statement best reflects the theme in this story?

   A. Punish crocodiles
   B. Keep the promises you make
   C. Look after young people
   D. Don't talk to strangers

5. In the passage, "Why the Crocodile has a Wide Mouth" the goddess of the water makes the crocodile's mouth stay open. What caused this to happen? Use 2 details from the text to support your answer.

6. In the passage, "Why the Crocodile has a Wide Mouth" the goddess of the water saves the boy's life. How does she save his life? How does she keep all of this information from the king of the land? Use 2 details from the text to support your answer.

WEEK 11

VIDEO
EXPLANATIONS

The Story of the Picture on the Vase

1. On some of the beautiful vases that are made in Japan there is a picture of a goddess changing a dragon into an island. When the children of Japan say, "Mother, tell us a story about the picture," this is what the mother says:

2. "Long, long ago there was a goddess of the sea who loved the people of Japan. She often came out of the water at sunset, and while all the bright colors were in the sky, she would sit on a high rock that overlooked the water and tell stories to the children. Such wonderful stories as they were! She used to tell them all about the strange fishes that swim in and out among the rocks, and about the fair maidens that live deep down in the sea far under the waves. The children would ask, 'Are there no children in the sea? Why do they never come out to play with us?' The goddess would answer, 'Some time they will come, if you only keep on wishing for them. What children really wish for they will surely have some day.'

3. "Then the goddess would sing to the children, and her voice was so sweet that the evening star would stand still in the sky to listen to her song. 'Please show us how the water rises and falls,' the children would beg, and she would hold up a magic stone that she had and say, 'Water, rise!' Then the waves would come in faster and faster all about the rock. When she laid down the stone and said, 'Water, fall!' the waves would be still, and the water would roll back quickly to the deep sea. She was goddess of the storm as well as of the sea, and sometimes the children would say, 'Dear goddess, please make us a storm.' She never said no to what they asked, and so the rain would fall, the lightning flare, and the thunder roll. The rain would fall all about them, but the goddess did not let it come near them. They were never afraid of the lightning, for it was far above their heads, and they knew that the goddess would not let it come down.

4. "Those were happy times, but there is something more to tell that is not pleasant. One of the goddess's sea-animals was a dragon, that often used to play in the water near the shore. The children never thought of being afraid of any of the sea-animals, but one day the cruel dragon seized a little child in his mouth, and in a moment he had eaten it. There was sadness over the land of Japan. There were tears and sorrowful wailing. 'O goddess,' the people cried, 'come to us! Punish the wicked dragon!'

5. "The goddess was angry that one of her creatures should have dared to harm the little child, and she called aloud, 'Dragon, come to me.' The dragon came in a moment, for he did not dare to stay away. Then said the goddess, 'You shall never again play merrily in the water with the happy sea-animals. You shall be a rocky island. There shall be trees and plants on you, and before many years have gone, people will no longer remember that you were once an animal.'

6. "The dragon found that he could no longer move about as he had done, for he was changing into rock. Trees and plants grew on his back. He was an island, and when people looked at it, they said, 'That island was once a wicked dragon.' The children of the sea and the children of the land often went to the island, and there they had very happy times together."

7. This is the story that the mothers tell to their children when they look at the vases and see the picture of the goddess changing a dragon into an island. But when the children say, "Mother, where is the island? Can't we go to it and play with the sea-children?" The mother answers, "Oh, this was all a long, long time ago, and no one can tell now where the island was."

When trying to determine who the narrator is carefully re-read the first few paragraphs and last few paragraphs for clues as to who might be telling the story.

Exercises

1. Who is the narrator in this story?

    A. The goddess of the sea
    B. The children in Japan
    C. The mother of the children in Japan
    D. The children of the goddess

Re-read this sentence from paragraph 4: "There were tears and sorrowful wailing."

4. Which is the best definition for the word sorrowful?

    A. Angry
    B. Sad
    C. Happy
    D. Annoyed

2. What do we learn about the goddess of the sea in paragraph 3?

    A. She is also the goddess of storms
    B. She is a cruel goddess
    C. She is also the goddess of the land
    D. She is the mother of the children

5. Which statement best describes the goddess of sea?

    A. She is a very angry person most of the time
    B. She is a forgetful person who barely remembers what the dragon has done
    C. She loves children and is usually sweet, becomes angry when the dragon hurts a child
    D. She loves the sea so much she doesn't pay attention to the children

3. Which best describes how paragraph 4 is related to paragraph 5?

    A. Paragraph 4 shows what the goddess does to the dragon for his actions and paragraph 5 shows the dragon's actions.
    B. Paragraph 4 shows the dragon's actions and paragraph 5 shows the goddess' response
    C. Paragraph 4 and 5 are not related
    D. Paragraph 4 explains what the children wanted to know and the paragraph 5 shows the mother telling the story

6. Why do you think the mother says, "Oh, this was all a long, long time ago, and no one can tell now where the island was." at the end of the story?

    A. Because it is the truth
    B. Because the island is too far away to get to reach
    C. Because the story she told is a myth and there really is no island
    D. Because she wants to keep the island a secret

How Flax Was Given to Men

1. "You have been on the mountain a long time," said the wife of the hunter.
2. "Yes, wife, and I have seen the most marvelous sight in all the world," replied the hunter.
3. "What was that?"
4. "I came to a place on the mountain where I had been many and many a time before, but a great hole had been made in the rock, and through the hole I saw—oh, wife, it was indeed a wonderful sight!"
5. "But what was it, my hunter?"
6. "There was a great hall, all shining and sparkling with precious stones. There were diamonds and pearls and emeralds, more than we could put into our little house, and among all the beautiful colors sat a woman who was fairer than they. Her maidens were around her, and the hall was as bright with their beauty as it was with the stones. One was playing on a harp, one was singing, and others were dancing as lightly and merrily as a sunbeam on a blossom. The woman was even more beautiful than the maidens, and, wife, as soon as I saw her I thought that she was no mortal woman."
7. "Did you not fall on your knees and ask her to be good to us?"
8. "Yes, wife, and straight way she said: 'Rise, my friend. I have a gift for you. Choose what you will to carry to your wife as a gift from Holda.'"
9. "Did you choose pearls or diamonds?"
10. "I looked about the place, and it was all so sparkling that I closed my eyes. 'Choose your gift,' she said. I looked into her face, and then I knew that it was indeed the goddess Holda, queen of the sky. When I looked at her, I could not think of precious stones, for her eyes were more sparkling than diamonds, and I said: 'O goddess Holda, there is no gift in all your magic hall that I would so gladly take away to my home as the little blue flower in your hand.'"
11. "Well!" cried the wife, "and when you might have had half the pearls and emeralds in the place, you chose a little faded blue flower! I did think you were a wiser man."
12. "The goddess said I had chosen well," said the hunter. "She gave me the flower and the seed of it, and she said, 'When the spring time comes, plant the seed, and in the summer I myself will come and teach you what to do with the plant.'"
13. In the spring the little seeds were put into the ground. Soon the green leaves came up; then many little blue flowers, as blue as the sky, lifted up their heads in the warm sunshine of summer. No one on the earth knew how to spin or to weave, but on the brightest, sunniest day of the summer, the goddess Holda came down from the mountain to the little house.
14. "Can you spin flax?" she asked of the wife.
15. "Indeed, no," said the wife.
16. "Can you weave linen?"
17. "Indeed, no."
18. "Then I will teach you how to spin and to weave," said the good goddess. "The little blue flower is the flax. It is my own flower, and I love the sight of it."
19. So the goddess sat in the home of the hunter and his wife and taught them how to spin flax and weave linen. When the wife saw the piece of linen on the grass, growing whiter and whiter the longer the sun shone upon it, she said to her husband, "Indeed, my hunter, the linen is fairer than the pearls, and I should rather have the beautiful white thing that is on the grass in the sunshine than all the diamonds in the hall of the goddess."

Think about cause and effect relationships as you read. More often than not there will be some type of cause and or effect question.

Exercises

Re-read this line from paragraph 6: "...and among all the beautiful colors sat a woman who was fairer than they."

1. Which best describes what the word farier means in this sentence?

   A. The woman followed the rules
   B. The woman was angry
   C. The woman was the most beautiful
   D. The woman was more ugly than the rest

2. Which statement shows why the hunter chose the flower?

   A. The hunter knew his wife would love the flower
   B. The hunter knew the value of the flower was more than the stones and jewels
   C. The hunter was so distracted by her beauty he couldn't focus on anything else
   D. The goddess told him to take the flower

3. Which best describes why the goddess returned to the hunter and his wife?

   A. To take back the seeds and flower
   B. Take make sure the seeds were growing
   C. To teach them how to make the flowers and seeds valuable by weaving and spinning it
   D. To make sure they were sharing their gift

4. Why does the wife change her mind at the end of the story?

   A. She is put under a spell by the goddess
   B. The hunter tricked her
   C. She realizes that the flower is more valuable than the stones
   D. She loves her husband regardless of what he chose

5. Which statement best reflects the theme in this passage?

   A. Don't be greedy
   B. Don't judge a book by its cover
   C. Love your husband / wife
   D. Do unto others as you want others to do unto you

6. Which of the following should be included in a summary of the story?

   A. A hunter fell into a hole and found some jewels but decided to take a flower instead
   B. A love story about a hunter and his wife
   C. A hunter finds a hall with a goddess, and he chooses and unlikely gift that turns out well
   D. A hunter and his wife fight over jewels and flowers

Ancient Man Deals with the Cold

1. Something was the matter with the weather. Early man did not know what "time" meant. He kept no records of birthdays and wedding-anniversaries or the hour of death. He had no idea of days or weeks or years. When the sun rose in the morning he did not say "Behold another day." He said "It is Light" and he used the rays of the early sun to gather food for his family.

2. When it grew dark, he returned to his wife and children, gave them part of the day's catch (some berries and a few birds), stuffed himself full with raw meat and went to sleep.

3. In a very general way he kept track of the seasons. Long experience had taught him that the cold Winter was invariably followed by the mild Spring -- that Spring grew into the hot Summer when fruits ripened and the wild ears of corn were ready to be plucked and eaten. The Summer ended when gusts of wind swept the leaves from the trees and when a number of animals crept into their holes to make ready for the long hibernal sleep.

4. It had always been that way. Early man accepted these useful changes of cold and warm but asked no questions. He lived and that was enough to satisfy him.

5. Suddenly, however, something happened that worried him greatly.

6. The warm days of Summer had come very late. The fruits had not ripened at all. The tops of the mountains which used to be covered with grass lay deeply hidden under a heavy burden of snow.

7. Then one morning quite a number of wild people, different from the other people of his valley had came from the land of the high peaks.

8. They muttered sounds which no one could understand. They looked lean and appeared to be starving. Hunger and cold seemed to have driven them from their former homes.

9. There was not enough food in the valley for both the old people who had been living there and the new comers. When they tried to stay more than a few days there was a terrible fight and whole families were killed. The others fled into the woods and were not seen again.

10. For a long time nothing occurred of any importance.

11. But all the while, the days grew shorter and the nights were colder than they should have been.

12. Finally, in a gap between the two high hills, there appeared a tiny speck of greenish ice. It grew in size as the years went by. Very slowly a gigantic glacier was sliding down the slopes of the mountain. Huge stones were being pushed into the valley. With the noise of a dozen thunderstorms they suddenly tumbled among the frightened people and killed them while they slept. 100 year-old trees were crushed into small pieces of wood by the high walls of ice.

13. At last, it began to snow.

14. It snowed for months and months and months.

15. All the plants died. The animals fled in search of the southern sun. The valley became unlivable. Man carried his children upon his back, took the few pieces of stone which he had used as a weapon and went forth to find a new home.

16. Why the world should have grown cold at that particular moment, we do not know. We can not even guess at the cause.

17. The gradual lowering of the temperature, however, made a great difference to the human race.

18. For a time it looked as if everyone would die. But in the end this period of suffering proved a real blessing. It killed all the weaker people and forced the survivors to sharpen their wits.

In short response answers be sure to answer the question in your own words before using evidence from the text to support what you have just said.

19. For example, there was the question of clothing. It had grown much too cold to do without some sort of artificial covering. Bears and bisons and other animals who live in northern regions are protected against snow and ice by a heavy coat of fur. Man possessed no such coat. His skin was very delicate and he suffered greatly.

20. He solved his problem in a very simple fashion. He dug a hole and he covered it with branches and leaves and a little grass. A bear came by and fell into this artificial cave. Man waited until the creature was weak from lack of food and then killed him with many blows of a big stone. With a sharp piece of rock he cut the fur of the animal's back. Then he dried it in the rare rays of the sun, put it around his own shoulders and enjoyed the same warmth that had formerly kept the bear happy and comfortable.

Exercises

Re-read paragraph 6.

1. What do you think the phrase, "heavy burden of snow." most likely means?

A. A small amount of heavy snow
B. A large amount of heavy snow
C. Hard to see snow that is very heavy
D. Snow that hurts people because it is heavy when it falls

Re-read paragraph 18.

3. What is the main reason the author includes this information?

A. To show that people were evil and killed each other in time of need
B. To describe how people survived
C. To explain what people did wrong during this time
D. To explain that some good things came from this time period

2. Which detail best shows why new people came to the valley when the cold period began?

A. The fruits had not ripened at all.
B. For a long time nothing occurred of any importance.
C. Hunger and cold seemed to have driven them from their former homes.
D. There was not enough food in the valley for both the old people who had been living there and the newcomers.

Read this lines from paragraph 12: "With the noise of a dozen thunderstorms..."

4. Why do you think the author included this phrase in the passage?

A. To show that there were thunderstorms
B. To explain how destructive the ice was
C. To describe how the people who lived there felt
D. He liked thunderstorms

5. In the passage "Ancient Man Deals with the Cold" man survives this cold period in time. How does he survive? Use 2 details from the text to support your answer.

6. In the passage "Ancient Man Deals with the Cold" the cause of the cold period is unknown, but the effects are told to us. What were some of the effects of the cold period? Use 2 details from the text to support your answer.

WEEK 12

VIDEO
EXPLANATIONS

ARGOPREP.COM

The Land of the Living and the Land of the Dead

1. The History of Man is the record of a hungry creature in search of food. Wherever food was plentiful and easily gathered, man travelled to make his home.

2. The fame of the Nile valley must have spread at an early date. From far and wide, wild people flocked to the banks of the river. Surrounded on all sides by desert or sea, it was not easy to reach these fields which were perfect for farming and living, and only the hardiest men and women survived.

3. We do not know who they were. Some came from the middle of Africa and had woolly hair and thick lips.

4. Others, with a yellowish skin, came from the desert of Arabia and the broad rivers of western Asia.

5. They fought each other for the possession of this wonderful land.

6. They built villages which their neighbors destroyed, and they rebuilt them with the bricks they had taken from other neighbors whom they in turn had destroyed.

7. Gradually a new race developed. They called themselves "remi," which means simply "the Men." There was a touch of pride in this name and they used it in the same sense that we refer to America as "God's own country."

8. Part of the year, during the annual flood of the Nile, they lived on small islands within a country which itself was cut off from the rest of the world by the sea and the desert. No wonder that these people were what we call "insular," and had the habits of villagers who rarely come in contact with their neighbors.

9. They liked their own ways best. They thought their own habits and customs were just a little better than those of anybody else. In the same way, their own gods were considered more powerful than the gods of other nations. They did not exactly hate others, but they felt a mild pity for them and if possible they kept them outside of the Egyptian lands. They were worried that their own people might be influenced in anegative way by "foreign notions."

10. They were kind-hearted and rarely did anything that was cruel. They were patient and in business dealings they didn't take sides when other people fought. Life came as an easy gift and they never became stingy and mean like northern people who have to struggle to live due to the cold conditions.

11. When the sun arose above the blood-red horizon of the distant desert, they went forth to work in their fields. When the last rays of light had disappeared beyond the mountain ridges, they went to bed.

12. They worked hard, and had a profound patience. They weren't lazy, but never stressed.

13. They believed that this life was but a short introduction to a new existence which began the moment Death had entered the house. Until at last, the life of the future came to be thought of as more important than the life of the present and the people of Egypt turned their booming land into one vast shrine for the worship of the dead.

14. And as most of the papyrus-rolls (ancient paper) of the ancient valley tell stories of a religious nature, we know with great truth just what gods the Egyptians believed in. They tried to make sure all possible happiness and comfort was given to those who had entered upon the eternal sleep (death). In the beginning each little village had possessed a god of its own.

15. Often this god was supposed to live in an oddly shaped stone or in the branch of a particularly large tree. It was well to be good friends with him for he could do great harm and destroy the harvest and prolong the period of drought until the people and the cattle had all died of thirst. Therefore the villages made him presents--offered him things to eat or a bunch of flowers.

16. When the Egyptians went forth to fight their enemies the god must be taken along, until he became a sort of battle flag around which the people rallied in time of danger.

Circle unknown or tricky words. If you need to understand this word to answer a question go back and figure out its meaning by using one of your strategies. If its not important for a question, move on!

17. But when the country grew older and better roads had been built and the Egyptians had begun to travel, the old beliefs lost their importance and were thrown away.

18. Their place was taken by new gods who were more powerful than the old ones had been and who represented those forces of nature which influenced the lives of the Egyptians of the entire valley.

Exercises

Re-read this phrase from paragraph 2: "...and only the hardiest men and women survived."

1. What do you think the word hardiest means in this phrase?

   A. Mean
   B. Tough
   C. Sad
   D. Hard to be around

2. Which best describes why villagers fought with each other before the new race of "Remi" people began?

   A. They didn't like people from other lands so they fought with them because they looked different
   B. They fought over belief in different gods
   C. The villagers were angry about the floods
   D. They fought over food and land

3. Which detail does not help you understand the word insular as it is used in paragraph 8?

   A. They liked their own ways best
   B. ...had the habits of villagers who rarely come in contact with their neighbors
   C. They worked hard, and had a profound patience
   D. ...they lived on small islands within a country which itself was cut off from the rest of the world by the sea and the desert

4. Which statement best describes the people of the nile?

   A. They were warriors
   B. They hated outsiders
   C. They liked their own ways best
   D. They believed in only 1 God

5. How did the villager's belief in gods change over time?

   A. At first they believed that gods live in nature that affected their life, then they believed that gods live that any kind of nature, even odd things
   B. At first they believed that gods live in any kind of nature even odd things, then they believed gods live in nature that affected their lives.
   C. At first they believed in 1 God then many gods
   D. At first they believed in many gods and then just 1 God

6. Why did the the villagers offer presents to the gods?

   A. To make sure that nature treated the people well
   B. To make sure that they had a comfortable and happy after-life
   C. To get presents back
   D. To help convince the gods that the people were the greatest on earth

How the Raven Helped Men

1. The raven and the eagle were cousins, and they were almost always friendly, but whenever they talked together about men, they quarreled.

2. "Men are lazy," declared the eagle. "There is no use in trying to help them. The more one does for them, the less they do for themselves."

3. "You fly so high," said the raven, "that you cannot see how hard men work. I think that we birds, who know so much more than they, ought to help them."

4. "They do not work," cried the eagle. "What have they to do, I should like to know? They walk about on the ground, and their food grows close by their nests. If they had to fly through the air as we do, and get their food wherever they could, they might talk about working hard."

5. "That is just why we ought to help them," replied the raven. "They cannot mount up into the air as we do. They cannot see anything very well unless it is near them, and if they had to run and catch their food, they would surely die of hunger. They are poor, weak creatures.

6. "You are a poor, weak bird, if you think you can teach men. When they feel hunger, they will eat, and they do not know how to do anything else. Just look at them! They ought to be going to sleep, and they do not know enough to do even that."

7. "How can they know that it is night, when they have no sun and no moon to tell them when it is day and when it is night?"

8. "They would not go to sleep even if they had two moons," said the eagle; "and you are no true cousin of mine if you do not let them alone."

9. So the two birds quarreled. Almost every time they met, they quarreled about men, and at last, whenever the eagle began to mount into the air, the raven went near the earth.

10. Now the eagle had a pretty daughter. She and the raven were good friends, and they never quarreled about men. One day the pretty daughter said, "Cousin Raven, are you too weak to fly as high as you used to do?"

11. "I never was less weak," declared the raven.

12. "Almost every day you keep on the ground. Can you not mount into the air?"

13. "Of course I can," answered the raven.

14. "There are some strange things in my father's lodge," said the pretty daughter, "and I do not know what they are. They are not good to eat, and I do not see what else they are good for. Will you come and see them?"

15. "I will go wherever you ask me," declared the raven.

16. The eagle's lodge was far up on the top of a high mountain, but the two birds were soon there, and the pretty daughter showed the raven the strange things. He knew what they were, and he said to himself, "Men shall have them, and by and then they will be no less wise than the birds." Then he asked, "Has your father a magic cloak?"

17. "Yes," answered the pretty daughter.

18. "May I put it on?"

19. "Yes, surely."

20. When the raven had once put on the magic cloak, he seized the strange things and put them under it. Then he called, "I will come again soon, my pretty little cousin, and tell you all about the people on the earth."

To better understand the story visualize what is happening. Picture the characters taking action to really get a deeper meaning of what is going on.

21.   The things under his cloak were strange indeed, for one was the sun, and one was the moon. There were hundreds of bright stars, and there were brooks and rivers and waterfalls. Best of all, there was the precious gift of fire. The raven put the sun high up in the heavens, and fastened the moon and stars in their places. He let the brooks run down the sides of the mountains, and he hid the fire away in the rocks.

22.   After a while men found all these precious gifts. They knew when it was night and when it was day, and they learned how to use fire. They cannot mount into the air like the eagle, but in some things they are almost as wise as the birds.

Exercises

1. What does the word quarreled mean as it is used in this passage?

   A. Fought with fists
   B. Fought with words
   C. Complimented each other
   D. Asked for help

2. Which best describes how the eagle feels about man?

   A. He thinks man could be smart if he had some help
   B. He thinks there is no helping man no matter the help he gets
   C. He thinks man is evil and they should fight with him
   D. He loves man

3. Which best describes how raven feels about man?

   A. He thinks man could be smart if he had some help
   B. He thinks there is no helping man no matter the help he gets
   C. He thinks man is evil and they should fight with him
   D. He hates man

5. Which best describes the raven?

   A. Stubborn
   B. Helpful
   C. Angry
   D. Stupid

4. Which should be included in a summary of this passage?

   A. Raven and eagle want to help man
   B. Eagle does everything he can to help man
   C. Raven and eagle fight about helping man, but the raven wants to help
   D. Raven and eagle fight about helping man, but eagle wants to help

6. Which is most likely the reason the eagle has the "strange things" in his home?

   A. He is saving them to help man
   B. He is hiding them as a gift to his daughter
   C. He is hiding them from man and the raven
   D. He is waiting to give the gifts to raven

 Find detailed video explanations to each problem on:
ArgoPrep.com

The Making of a State

1. Nowadays we all are members of a "state."
2. We may be Frenchmen or Americans or Russians; we may live in the furthest corner of Indonesia, but in some way or another we belong to that curious combination of people which is called the "state."
3. It does not matter whether we recognize a king or an emperor or a president as our ruler. We are born and we die as a small part of this large whole and no one can escape this fate.
4. The "state," as a matter of fact, is quite a recent invention.
5. The earliest inhabitants of the world did not know what it was.
6. Every family lived and hunted and worked and died for and by itself. Sometimes it happened that a few of these families, for the sake of greater protection against the wild animals and against other wild people, formed a loose alliance which was called a tribe or a clan. But as soon as the danger was past, these groups of people acted again by and for themselves and if the weak could not defend their own cave, they were left to the mercies of the hyena and the tiger and nobody was very sorry if they were killed.
7. In short, each person was a nation unto himself and he felt no responsibility for the happiness and safety of his neighbor. Very, very slowly this was changed and Egypt was the first country where the people were organized into a well-run empire.
8. The Nile was directly responsible for this useful development. In the summer of each year the greater part of the Nile valley and the Nile delta is turned into a vast inland sea due to flooding. To get the greatest benefit from this water and yet survive the flood, it had been necessary at certain points to build dams and small islands which would offer shelter for man and beast during the months of August and September. The construction of these little artificial islands however had not been simple.
9. A single man or a single family or even a small tribe could not construct a river-dam without the help of others.
10. However much a farmer might dislike his neighbors he disliked getting drowned even more. So he had to call upon the entire country-side for help when the water of the river began to rise and threatened him and his wife and his children and his cattle with destruction.
11. Need forced the people to forget their small differences and soon the entire valley of the Nile was covered with little combinations of people who constantly worked together for a common purpose and who depended upon each other for life and happiness.
12. Out of such small beginnings grew the first powerful state.
13. It was a great step forward along the road of progress.
14. It made the land of Egypt a truly awesome place to live. It meant the end of lawless crimes. It assured the people greater safety than ever before and gave the weaker members of the tribe a chance to survive. Nowadays it is hard to imagine a world without laws and policemen and judges and health officers and hospitals and schools.
15. But five thousand years ago, Egypt stood alone as an organized state and was greatly looked up to by those of her neighbors who were forced to face the difficulties of life single-handedly.
16. A state, however, is not only composed of citizens.

 **TIP** of the **DAY**

By previewing the questions you can determine the most important parts of the story and really take your time and read those parts more carefully. Determining importance can save you a lot of time!

17. There must be a few men who make and carry out the laws and who, in case of an emergency, take command of the entire community. Therefore no country has ever been able to last without a single head, be he called a King or an Emperor or a President, as he is called in our own land.

18. In ancient Egypt, every village recognized the authority of the Village-Elders, who were old men and possessed greater experience than the young ones. These Elders selected a strong man to command their soldiers in case of war and to tell them what to do when there was a flood. They gave him a title which made him different from the others. They called him a King or a prince and obeyed his orders for their own common benefit.

Exercises

1. What is the meaning of "inhabitants" as it is used in paragraph 5?

   A. Wild animals
   B. Pets
   C. People
   D. None of the above

2. Which best describes the direct cause of the creation of the first state?

   A. Farmers were at war with each other and needed protection
   B. The nile was flooding so farmers needed to rely on each other for help to build safe homes
   C. Outsiders were causing harm to farmers so they came together to form a state
   D. The need for a ruler was the main reason farmers formed a state

3. Before the first state which best describes how farmers survived?

   A. Farmers helped each other when they absolutely had to, but then went back to living their own lives, looking out for themselves only
   B. Farmers were already coming together to fight off enemies and decided it was best to just stick together all the time even after the enemies had left
   C. Farmers always looked out for themselves and never helped others
   D. Farmers were violent people who fought with their neighbors just to survive

4. Which statement is true about how they selected leaders for the first state?

   A. They voted democratically
   B. The village elders were trusted to lead and chose a leader in time of war
   C. There were no leaders
   D. Leaders were given a chance, but if they failed in war they were fired

5. In the passage "The Making of a State" there were many advantages to people creating the first state. What were some of those advantages? Use 2 details from the text to support your answer.

6. In the passage "The Making of a State" the author describes what goes into making a state. Describe some of the things that make up a state. Use 2 details from the text to support your answer.

WEEK 13

VIDEO
EXPLANATIONS

ARGOPREP.COM

 Find detailed video explanations to each problem on:
ArgoPrep.com

Greek Self-Government

1. In the beginning, all the Greeks had been equally rich and equally poor. Every man had owned a certain number of cows and sheep. His mud-hut had been his castle. He had been free to come and go as he wished. Whenever it was needed to discuss matters of public importance, all the citizens had gathered in the market-place. One of the older men of the village was elected chairman and it was his duty to see that everybody had a chance to express their views. In case of war, a particularly energetic and self confident villager was chosen commander-in-chief, but the same people who had given this man the right to be their leader, had an equal right to take away this job.

2. But gradually the village had grown into a city. Some people had worked hard and others had been lazy. A few had been unlucky and still others had been just plain dishonest in dealing with their neighbors and had gained wealth. As a result, the city no longer consisted of a number of men who were equally well-off. On the contrary it was lived in by a small class of very rich people and a large class of very poor ones.

3. There had been another change. The old commander-in-chief who had been known as "headman" or "King" because he knew how to lead his men to victory, had disappeared from the scene. His place had been taken by the nobles—a class of rich people who during the course of time had got hold of an unfair share of the farms and estates.

4. These nobles enjoyed many advantages over the common crowd of freemen. They were able to buy the best weapons. They had much spare time in which they could practice the art of fighting. They lived in strongly built houses and they could hire soldiers to fight for them. They were constantly fighting among each other to decide who should rule the city. The nobleman that won then assumed a sort of Kingship over all his neighbors and governed the town until he in turn was killed or driven away by still another ambitious nobleman.

5. The people of Athens (a large city in Greece) decided to do some house cleaning and give the large number of freemen once more a voice in the government as they were supposed to have had in the days of their ancestors. They asked a man by the name of Draco to provide them with a set of laws that would protect the poor against the aggressions of the rich. Draco set to work. Unfortunately he was very much out of touch with ordinary life. In his eyes a crime was a crime and when he had finished his code, the people of Athens discovered that these Draconian laws were so harsh that they could not be put into effect.

6. The Athenians looked about for a more gentle reformer. At last they found someone who could do that sort of thing better than anybody else. His name was Solon. He belonged to a noble family and he had travelled all over the world and had studied the forms of government of many other countries. After a careful study of the subject, Solon gave Athens a set of laws which stayed true to that wonderful idea of moderation (not too strict, but not too easy) which was part of the Greek character. He tried to improve the condition of the poor man without destroying the wealth of the nobles who were of such great service to the state as soldiers. To protect the poorer classes against wrong-doing on the part of the judges (who were always elected from the class of the nobles because they received no salary) Solon made a provision where by a citizen with a problem or complaint had the right to state his case before a jury of thirty of his fellow Athenians.

 *When a text is difficult to understand break it down in chunks. Re-state the main idea of each chunk and write it down so you can go back and find information easier later.*

7. Most important of all, Solon forced the average freeman to take a direct and personal interest in the affairs of the city. No longer could he stay at home and say "oh, I am too busy today" or "it is raining and I had better stay indoors." He was expected to do his share; to be at the meeting of the town council; and carry part of the responsibility for the safety and the moneymaking of the state.

8. This government by the the people was often unsuccessful. But it taught the Greek people to be independent and to rely upon themselves for their happiness and health and that was a very good thing.

Exercises

1. Which statement is true about the Greek villages before they turned into cities?

   A. Men were mostly equal in wealth and property
   B. Some men were very rich while others were very poor
   C. Some men worked hard while others were lazy
   D. Most men were very poor

2. What does the word noble mean as it is used in this passage?

   A. To good the right thing
   B. A very poor person
   C. A king
   D. A small group of men who had money and power

3. What is the main difference between the Draco laws and the Solon laws?

   A. Draco's laws were too easy on man while Solon's laws were too harsh
   B. Solon's laws were just right for poor and rich men but Draco's laws were too harsh
   C. Draco's laws favored the poor man and Solon's laws favored the rich man
   D. Solon's laws didn't punish anyone while Draco's laws punished everyone

4. Which best describes the villagers when the village grew into a city?

   A. All of the men grew lazy
   B. All of the men became rich
   C. All of the men became thieves
   D. Some men were lazy, some were rich and some were dishonest

5. How did Solon's laws help the poor?

   A. He gave the poor a voice by allowing them to voice their concerns
   B. He lowered their taxes
   C. He gave them jobs
   D. He made sure people helped them out

6. Which statement would you include in a summary of this passage?

   A. The Greek people were so unhappy the needed a new kind of rule
   B. Life changed for the Greeks when their village grew so they needed a new set of laws
   C. Draco the first ruler was an important figure in the Greek government
   D. Nobles were kind men who looked out for the poor

Why the Woodpecker's Head is Red

1. One day the woodpecker said to the Great Spirit, "Men do not like me. I wish they did."
2. The Great Spirit said, "If you wish men to love you, you must be good to them and help them. Then they will call you their friend."
3. "How can a little bird help a man?" asked the woodpecker.
4. "If one wishes to help, the day will come when he can help," said the Great Spirit. The day did come, and this story shows how a little bird helped a strong warrior.
5. There was once a cruel magician who lived in a gloomy wigwam beside the Black-Sea-Water. He did not like flowers, and they did not blossom in his pathway. He did not like birds, and they did not sing in the trees above him. The breath of his nostrils was fatal to all life. North, south, east, and west he blew the deadly fever that killed the women and the little children.
6. "Can I help them?" thought a brave warrior, and he said, "I will find the magician, and see if death will not come to him as he has made it come to others. I will go straight way to his home."
7. For many days the brave warrior was in his canoe traveling across the Black-Sea-Water. At last he saw the gloomy wigwam of the cruel magician. He shot an arrow at the door and called, "Come out, O coward! You have killed women and children with your fatal breath, but you cannot kill a warrior. Come out and fight, if you are not afraid."
8. The cruel magician laughed loud and long. "One breath of fever," he said, "and you will fall to the earth." The warrior shot again, and then the magician was angry. He did not laugh, but he came straight out of his gloomy lodge, and as he came, he blew the fever all about him.
9. Then was seen the greatest fight that the sun had ever looked upon. The brave warrior shot his flint-tipped arrows, but the magician had on his magic cloak, and the arrows could not wound him. He blew from his nostrils the deadly breath of fever, but the heart of the warrior was so strong that the fever could not kill him.
10. At last the brave warrior had but three arrows in his quiver. "What shall I do?" he said sadly. "My arrows are good and my aim is good, but no arrow can go through the magic cloak."
11. "Come on, come on," called the magician. "You are the man who wished to fight. Come on." Then a woodpecker in a tree above the brave warrior said softly, "Aim your arrow at his head, O warrior! Do not shoot at his heart, but at the crest of feathers on his head. He can be wounded there, but not in his heart."
12. The warrior was not so proud that he could not listen to a little bird. The magician bent to lift a stone, and an arrow flew from the warrior's bow. It buzzed and stung like a wasp. It came so close to the crest of feathers that the magician trembled with terror. Before he could run, another arrow came, and this one struck him right on his head. His heart grew cold with fear. "Death has struck me," he cried.
13. "Your cruel life is over," said the warrior. "People shall no longer fear your fatal breath. "Then he said to the woodpecker, "Little bird, you have been a good friend to me, and I will do all that I can for you." He put some of the red blood of the magician upon the little creature's head. It made the group of feathers there as red as flame. "Whenever a man looks upon you," said the warrior, "he will say, 'That bird is our friend. He helped to kill the cruel magician.'"
14. The little woodpecker was very proud of his red head because it showed that he was the friend of man, and all his children to this day are as proud as he was.

Better understand the story by making predictions before you read and while you read. Even if your predictions are incorrect you are engaging with the text more closely.

Exercises

Re-read lines 1 and 2.

1. What is the main reason the author starts the passage this way?

   A. To show that man doesn't like birds
   B. To show that the bird wants to do something to become the friend of man
   C. To explain why man doesn't like birds
   D. None of the above

2. What do we learn about the magician in paragraph 5?

   A. He uses his powers to help others
   B. He likes birds
   C. He is evil
   D. He doesn't know how to control his powers

3. Which statement best describes the brave warrior?

   A. He is a brave warrior, but he fights the magician only for reward money
   B. The warrior just wants to protect the bird
   C. The warrior was scared before, but has grown into a brave man
   D. The warrior wants to kill the magician for the harm he has done

4. What does the word quiver mean as it is used in the sentence, "At last the brave warrior had but three arrows in his quiver."

   A. Heart
   B. Belt for carrying arrows
   C. Life
   D. Soldiers

5. Which best describes why the woodpecker's head is red?

   A. The woodpecker accidently got the magician blood on his head during the fight
   B. The woodpecker was hurt during the fight and it was his blood
   C. The warrior put some of the magician's blood on the woodpecker's head as a symbol of his thanks
   D. The warrior put blood on the woodpecker's head because he was angry with him

6. What is the main reason the woodpecker felt proud at the end of the story?

   A. His head was a beautiful red color
   B. He had helped man
   C. The magician was dead
   D. He had children of his own

An excerpt from **The Wizard of Oz**

1. Uncle Henry sat upon the doorstep and looked nervously at the sky, which was even grayer than usual. Dorothy stood in the door with Toto in her arms, and looked at the sky too. Aunt Em was washing the dishes.

2. From the far north they heard a low howl of the wind, and Uncle Henry and Dorothy could see where the long grass bent in waves before the coming storm. There now came a loud whistling in the air from the south, and as they turned their eyes that way they saw ripples in the grass coming from that direction also.

3. Suddenly Uncle Henry stood up.

4. "There's a cyclone coming, Em," he called to his wife. "I'll go look after the stock." Then he ran toward the sheds where the cows and horses were kept.

5. Aunt Em dropped her work and came to the door. One look told her of the danger close at hand.

6. "Quick, Dorothy!" she screamed. "Run for the basement!"

7. Toto jumped out of Dorothy's arms and hid under the bed, and the girl started to get him. Aunt Em, badly frightened, threw open the trap door in the floor and climbed down the ladder into the small, dark hole. Dorothy caught Toto at last and started to follow her aunt. When she was halfway across the room there came a great noise from the wind, and the house shook so hard that she lost her footing and fell down suddenly upon the floor.

8. Then a strange thing happened.

9. The house whirled around two or three times and rose slowly through the air. Dorothy felt as if she were going up in a balloon.

10. The north and south winds met where the house stood, and made it the exact center of the cyclone. In the middle of a cyclone the air is usually still, but the great pressure of the wind on every side of the house raised it up higher and higher, until it was at the very top of the cyclone; and there it remained and was carried miles and miles away as easily as you could carry a feather.

11. It was very dark, and the wind howled horribly around her, but Dorothy found she was riding quite easily. After the first few whirls around, and one other time when the house tipped badly, she felt as if she were being rocked gently, like a baby in a cradle.

12. Toto did not like it. He ran about the room, now here, now there, barking loudly; but Dorothy sat quite still on the floor and waited to see what would happen.

13. Once Toto got too near the open trap door, and fell in; and at first the little girl thought she had lost him. But soon she saw one of his ears sticking up through the hole, for the strong pressure of the air was keeping him up so that he could not fall. She crept to the hole, caught Toto by the ear, and dragged him into the room again, and closed the trap door so that no more accidents could happen.

14. Hour after hour passed away, and slowly Dorothy got over her fear; but she felt quite lonely, and the wind howled so loudly all about her that she nearly became deaf. At first she had wondered if she would be dashed to pieces when the house fell again; but as the hours passed and nothing terrible happened, she stopped worrying and resolved to wait calmly and see what the future would bring. At last she crawled over the swaying floor to her bed, and lay down upon it; and Toto followed and lay down beside her.

15. In spite of the swaying of the house and the wailing of the wind, Dorothy soon closed her eyes and fell fast asleep.

Better understand the text by making connections. You can make connections to other texts, yourself or other things in the world.

Exercises

Re-read paragraphs 1 and 2.

1. What is the author's main purpose for beginning the passage this way?

   A. To introduce the characters
   B. To show the setting
   C. To give background on the events
   D. To show who the narrator is

2. Which detail best helps you understand what the word stock means?

   A. "There's a cyclone coming"
   B. "Run for the basement!"
   C. Then he ran toward the sheds where the cows and horses were kept.
   D. Dorothy caught Toto

3. Why didn't Dorothy go into the basement with the rest of her family?

   A. She fell on the way to the trap door and didn't make it in time
   B. They locked her out on purpose
   C. She thought it would be safer to stay in her bedroom
   D. Toto showed her a safer place to be

4. Which best explains why Dorothy's house didn't fall in the cyclone?

   A. The house had magical powers
   B. The equal and strong wind pressure from all sides held the house up in the middle
   C. The house was light as a feather
   D. Dorothy used her magic powers to keep the house from falling

5. In the passage from "The Wizard of Oz" Dorothy is the main character. What kind of person is she? Use 2 details from the passage to support your answer.

6. In the passage from "The Wizard of Oz" Dorothy's house is taken away in a cyclone. What happens once the house is in the cyclone? Describe at least 2 events. Be sure to use 2 details from the passage to support your answer.

WEEK 14

VIDEO
EXPLANATIONS

ARGOPREP.COM

Julius Caesar

1. Nearly two thousand years ago there was a brave captain whose name was Julius Caesar. He led the army of the Roman Empire. The soldiers he led to battle were very strong, and they won battles against the people they fought, wherever they went.

2. They had no gun or gunpowder then; but they had swords and spears, and, to keep themselves from being hurt, they had helmets or golden caps on their heads, with long strands of horsehair on them. They also had body armor made of brass on their chests, and on their arms they carried a sort of shield, made of strong leather. One of them carried a little brass figure of an eagle on a long pole, with a red flag flying below, and wherever the eagle was seen, they all followed, and fought so bravely that nothing could long stand against them.

3. When Julius Caesar rode at their front, with his charming yet, pale hook-nosed face, and the red cloak that the general always wore, they were so proud of him, and so happy to have him as their leader, that there was nothing they would not do for him.

4. Julius Caesar heard that a little way off there was a country nobody knew anything about, except that the people were very fierce and savage, and that a sort of pearl was found in the shells of mussels which lived in the rivers. He could not stand that there should be any place that his own people, the Romans, did not know and rule. He was a man who had big dreams of ruling the whole world! So he ordered the ships to be prepared, and his soldiers to be ready, and soon enough, they set out to take this land and its people.

5. When he came quite close up to them, he found the savages were there in small numbers. They were tall men, with long red streaming hair, and the clothes they had were made of wool, and checked like plaid; but many had their arms and chests with nothing on them but were painted all over in blue patterns. They yelled and held their darts high, to make Julius Caesar and his Roman soldiers keep away; but he only went on to a place where the shore was not quite so steep, and there Caesar commanded his soldiers to land.

6. The savages had run along the shore too, and there was a terrible fight; but at last the man who carried the eagle jumped down into the middle of the natives, calling out to his fellows that they must come after him, or they would lose their eagle. They all came rushing and leaping down, and thus they managed to force back the savages, and make their way to the shore.

7. There was not much worth having when they had made their way there. Though they came again the next year, and forced their way a good deal farther into the country, they saw forests and woods only. The few houses that were there were little more than piles of stones, and the people were rough and wild, and could do very little. The men hunted wild boars, and wolves. The women dug the ground, and raised a little corn, which they ground to flour between two stones to make bread; and they spun the wool of their sheep, dyed it with bright colors, and wove it into dresses. They had some strong places in the woods, with trunks of trees, cut down to shut them in from the enemy, with all their flocks and cattle; but Caesar did not get into any of these. He only made the natives give him some of their pearls, and call the Romans their masters, and then he went back to his ships, and none of the people in the country saw Caesar or his Romans any more.

8. Do you know who these savages were who fought with Julius Caesar? They were called Britons. And the country he came to see? That was the very popular island, England, only it was not called so then.

Use any prior knowledge you have to help you better understand the text. Be careful not to use your own knowledge over what you have read in the text as evidence to back up your answer choices.

Exercises

1. Which of the following could be a subheading for paragraph 2?

    A. Meet Julius Caesar
    B. What the soldiers wore and how they defended themselves
    C. What the Roman Empire looked liked
    D. The beginning of the Roman Empire

2. Which best describes how the soldiers felt about Caesar?

    A. They loved him and would do anything for him
    B. The hated him and but did as he said
    C. They hated him and did not obey his orders
    D. They thought he was a good leader but didn't follow all of his orders

3. Why did Caesar want to take over this new country?

    A. He wanted their many natural resources
    B. He wanted the pearls from the mussels
    C. He loved the people and wanted to help them
    D. He wanted to rule everywhere and everything

4. What does the word savage or savages mean as it is used in this passage?

    A. Happy people
    B. Uncontrolled and angry
    C. Sad and lonely
    D. Rich People

5. Which statement best describes how Caesar and his soldiers found the savages living?

    A. They were living rich lives in big houses
    B. They were living simple hard-working lives in poor houses
    C. They were living in caves in the wild
    D. They were living in poor houses but had a lot of money

6. Which of the following belongs in a summary of the passage?

    A. Caesar and his army invade a country, because they want to rule the world
    B. Caesar helps a country to survive by taking it over
    C. A country fights with Caesar and wins
    D. Caesar invades a country and takes all of its goods

The Tiger, the Brahman, and the Jackal

1. Once upon a time, a tiger was caught in a trap. He tried in vain to get out through the bars, and rolled and bit with rage and grief when he failed.

2. By chance a poor Brahman (a religious man) came by. "Let me out of this cage, oh kind one!" cried the tiger.

3. "Nay, my friend," replied the Brahman mildly, "you would probably eat me if I did."

4. "Not at all!" swore the tiger with many promises; "quite the opposite, I should be forever grateful, and serve you as a slave!"

5. Now when the tiger sobbed and sighed and wept and swore, the kind Brahman's heart softened, and at last he agreed to open the door of the cage. Out popped the tiger, and, grabbing the poor man, cried, "What a fool you are! What is to stop me from eating you now, for after being stuck for so long I am just terribly hungry!"

6. In fear the Brahman pleaded for his life; but the most he could gain was a promise by the tiger. The promise was this; The brahman would ask three things if the tiger's action was fair and no matter what the three things said, the tiger had to listen.

7. So the Brahman first asked a pipal tree what it thought of the matter, but the pipal tree replied coldly, "What have you to complain about? Don't I give shade and shelter to everyone who passes by, and don't they in return tear down my branches to feed their cattle? Don't whimper—be a man!"

8. Then the Brahman, sad at heart, went further out till he saw a buffalo turning a wellwheel; but his answer was no better, for it answered, "You are a fool to expect anything else! Look at me! While I gave milk they fed me on cotton-seed and oil-cake, but now I am dry they sit me here, and give me garbage as food!"

9. The Brahman, still more sad, asked the road to give him its opinion.

10. "My dear sir," said the road, "how foolish you are to expect anything else! Here am I, useful to everybody, yet all, rich and poor, great and small, trample on me as they go past, giving me nothing but the ashes of their pipes!"

11. After this the Brahman turned back sadly, and on the way he met a jackal, who called out, "Why, what's the matter, Mr. Brahman? You look as miserable as a fish out of water!"

12. The Brahman told him all that had occurred. "How very confusing!" said the jackal, when the story had ended; "would you mind telling me over again, for everything has got so mixed up?"

13. The Brahman told it all over again, but the jackal shook his head in a distracted sort of way, and still could not understand.

14. "It's very odd," said he, sadly, "but it all seems to go in at one ear and out at the other! I will go to the place where it all happened, and then maybe I shall be able to give a you an opinion."

15. So they returned to the cage, where the tiger was waiting for the Brahman. He was sharpening his teeth and claws.

16. "You've been away a long time!" growled the savage beast, "but now let us begin our dinner."

17. "Our dinner!" thought the frightened Brahman, as his knees knocked together with fright; "what a remarkably delicate way of putting it!"

Infer what characters are doing. Why is the Jackal acting this way? The text doesn't say it but you should know what he is up to, because you can infer!

18. "Give me five minutes, my lord!" he pleaded, "in order that I may explain things to the jackal here, who is somewhat slow in his wits."

19. The tiger agreed, and the Brahman began the whole story over again, not missing a single detail.

20. "Oh, my poor brain! Oh, my poor brain!" cried the jackal, rubbing its paws. "Let me see! How did it all begin? You were in the cage, and the tiger came walking by—"

21. "Pooh!" interrupted the tiger, "what a fool you are! I was in the cage."

22. "Of course!" cried the jackal, pretending to tremble with fright; "yes! I was in the cage—no I wasn't—dear! dear! where are my wits? Let me see—the tiger was in the Brahman, and the cage came walking by—no, that's not it, either! Well, don't mind me, but begin your dinner, for I shall never understand!"

23. "Yes, you shall!" returned the tiger, in a rage at the jackal's stupidity; "I'll make you understand! Look here—I am the tiger—"

24. "Yes, my lord!"

25. "And that is the Brahman—"

26. "Yes, my lord!"

27. "And that is the cage—"

28. "Yes, my lord!"

29. "And I was in the cage—do you understand?"

30. "Yes—no—Please, my lord—"

31. "Well?" cried the tiger impatiently.

32. "Please, my lord!—how did you get in?"

33. "How!—why in the usual way, of course!"

34. "Oh, dear me!—my head is beginning to whirl again! Please don't be angry, my lord, but what is the usual way?"

35. At this the tiger lost patience, and, jumping into the cage, cried, "This way! Now do you understand how it was?"

36. "Perfectly!" grinned the jackal, as he quickly shut the door, "and if you will allow me to say so, I think things will remain as they were!"

Exercises

1. What happens in paragraph 5 that sets the stage for the rest of the story?

   A. The brahman helps the tiger and the tiger is grateful
   B. The brahman helps the tiger and we learn the tiger is untruthful
   C. The brahman doesn't help the tiger, but the tiger escapes
   D. To show who the narrator is

4. Which statement best describes how the Jackal helps the Brahman?

   A. The Jackal's foolishness actually helps the Brahman in the end
   B. The Jackal pretends to be a fool to trick the tiger and help the Brahman
   C. The Jackal makes a deal with the Tiger to free the Brahman
   D. The Jackal never actually helps the Brahman

3. Which detail doesn't show why the three things don't feel bad for the Brahman?

   A. Here am I, useful to everybody, yet all, rich and poor, great and small, trample on me as they go past, giving me nothing but the ashes of their pipes!"
   B. Don't I give shade and shelter to everyone who passes by, and don't they in return tear down my branches to feed their cattle?
   C. While I gave milk they fed me on cotton-seed and oil-cake, but now I am dry they sit me here, and give me garbage as food!"
   D. "Why, what's the matter, Mr. Brahman? You look as miserable as a fish out of water!"

Re-read paragraph 17. "Our dinner!" thought the frightened Brahman, as his knees knocked together with fright; "what a remarkably delicate way of putting it!"

5. What does the author mean by, "what a remarkably delicate way of putting it!"?

   A. The tiger was actually delicate when telling the Brahman of his fate
   B. The tiger was quite harsh when saying this and the Brahman was being sarcastic
   C. The tiger knew the Brahman would be a delicate meal
   D. The Brahman was thankful that the tiger had told him of his fate in this way

2. Which detail from the text best shows how the three things felt about the Brahman's story?

   A. "Don't whimper—be a man!"
   B. "You've been away a long time!"
   C. "You look as miserable as a fish out of water!"
   D. "It's very odd,"

6. Which of the following is a theme or moral in the story?

   A. Don't trust tigers
   B. Smarts and wits and stronger than power and might
   C. Don't be nice to strangers
   D. Be kind to strangers

Find detailed video explanations to each problem on:
ArgoPrep.com

How the Rabbit Lost His Tail

1. Once upon a time, ages and ages ago, the rabbit had a long tail, but the cat had none. She looked with jealous eyes at the one which the rabbit had. It was exactly the sort of a tail she longed to have.

2. The rabbit was always a thoughtless, careless little beast. One day he went to sleep with his beautiful long tail hanging straight out behind him. Along came Mistress Puss carrying a sharp knife, and with one blow she cut off Mr. Rabbit's tail. Mistress Puss was very sneaky and she had the tail nearly sewed on to her own body before Mr. Rabbit saw what she was doing.

3. "Don't you think it looks better on me than it did on you?" asked Mistress Puss.

4. "It surely is very becoming to you," replied the generous, unselfish rabbit. "It was a little too long for me anyway and I'll tell you what I'll do. I'll let you keep it if you will give me that sharp knife in exchange for it."

5. The cat gave Mr. Rabbit the knife and he started out into the deep forest with it. "I've lost my tail but I've gained a knife," said he; "I'll get a new tail or something else just as good."

6. Mr. Rabbit hopped along through the forest for a long time and at last he came to a little old man who was busily focused in making baskets. He was making the baskets out of leaves and sticks and he was biting them off with his teeth. He looked up and spied Mr. Rabbit with the knife in his mouth.

7. "O, please, Mr. Rabbit," said he, "will you not be so kind as to let me borrow that sharp knife you are carrying? It is very hard work to bite the leaves and sticks off with my teeth."

8. Mr. Rabbit let him take the knife. He started to cut off the sticks with it, when snap went the knife! It broke into halves.

9. "O, dear! O, dear!" cried Mr. Rabbit. "What shall I do! What shall I do! You have broken my nice new knife."

10. The little old man said that he was very sorry and that he did not mean to do it.

11. Then Mr. Rabbit said, "A broken knife is of no use to me but perhaps you can use it, even if it is broken. I'll tell you what I'll do. I'll let you keep the knife if you will give me one of your baskets in exchange for it."

12. The little old man gave Mr. Rabbit a basket and he started on through the deep forest with it. "I lost my tail but I gained a knife. I've lost my knife but I've gained a basket," said he. "I'll get a new tail or something else just as good."

13. Mr. Rabbit hopped along through the deep forest for a long time until at last he came to a clearing. Here there was an old woman busily working in picking lettuce. When she had gathered it she put it into her apron. She looked up and spied Mr. Rabbit hopping along with his basket.

14. "O, please, Mr. Rabbit," said she, "will you not be so kind as to let me borrow that nice basket you are carrying?"

15. Mr. Rabbit let her take the basket. She began to put her lettuce into it when out fell the bottom of the basket.

16. "O, dear! O, dear!" cried Mr. Rabbit. "What shall I do! What shall I do! You have broken the bottom out of my nice new basket."

17. The old woman said that she was very sorry and that she did not mean to do it.

TIP of the DAY

Ask questions about what characters are doing things. Try to answer them as you read on. Doing this can help you better understand character's motivations.

18. Then said Mr. Rabbit, "I'll tell you what I'll do. I'll let you keep that broken basket if you will give me some of your lettuce."

19. The old woman gave Mr. Rabbit some lettuce and he hopped along with it, saying, "I lost my tail but I gained a knife. I lost my knife but I gained a basket. I lost my basket but I gained some lettuce."

20. The rabbit was getting very hungry and how nice the lettuce smelled! He took a bite. It was just the very best thing he had ever tasted in all his life. "I don't care if I did lose my tail," said he, "I've found something I like very much better."

21. From that day to this no rabbit has ever had a tail. Neither has there ever been a rabbit who cared because he had no tail. From that time to this there has never been a rabbit who did not like lettuce to eat and who was not perfectly happy and contented if there was plenty of it.

Exercises

1. Which best describes how the cat got the rabbit's tail?

   A. The rabbit gave it to the cat in a trade for his knife
   B. The cat stole the rabbit's tail when it was sleeping
   C. The rabbit thought the cat wanted the tail so he gave it to him for free
   D. The cat asked the rabbit for his tail

Re-read this line from paragraph 4: "I'll let you keep it if you will give me that sharp knife in exchange for it."

2. What does the word **exchange** mean in this sentence?

   A. Give it back
   B. Trade
   C. Money
   D. Stolen

3. Which best describes the theme of this passage?

   A. Make the best of what you have
   B. Don't trade with animals
   C. Make sure you share your things for free
   D. Don't get tricked by sneaky animals

4. Which best describes the rabbit?

   A. A sneaky rabbit who tricks animals into giving him better things
   B. A mean rabbit that steals gifts from others
   C. A kind rabbit who is wise and makes trades to help himself and others
   D. A stupid rabbit that doesn't realize the animals are tricking him

5. In the story "How the Rabbit Lost His Tail" the rabbit trades with the other animals. Name 2 things he trades for and why he does it. Be sure to use details from the text to support your answer.

6. In the story "How the Rabbit Lost His Tail" the rabbit is the main character. What kind of person is the rabbit? Why do you think that he is this way? Be sure to use details from the text to support your answer.

WEEK 15

VIDEO EXPLANATIONS

ARGOPREP.COM

How a Prince Learned to Read

1. A thousand years ago boys and girls did not learn to read. Books were very scarce and very precious, and only a few men could read them.

2. Each book was written with a pen or a brush. The pictures were painted by hand, and some of them were very beautiful. A good book would sometimes cost as much as a good house.

3. In those times there were even some kings who could not read. They thought more of hunting and fighting than of learning.

4. There was one such king who had four sons, Ethelbald, Ethelbert, Ethelred, and Alfred

5. The three older boys were strong, half-grown lads; the youngest, Alfred, was a skinny, fair-haired child.

6. One day when they were with their mother, she showed them a wonderful book that some rich friend had given her. She turned the pages and showed them the strange letters. She showed them the beautiful pictures, and told them how they had been drawn and painted.

7. They liked the book very much, for they had never seen anything like it. "But the best part of it is the story which it tells," said their mother. "If you could only read, you might learn that story and enjoy it. Now I want to give this book to one of you"

8. "Will you give it to me, mother?" asked little Alfred.

9. "I will give it to the one who first learns to read in it" she answered.

10. "I am sure I would rather have a good bow with arrows" said Ethelred.

11. "And I would rather have a young hawk that has been trained to hunt" said Ethelbert.

12. "If I were a priest or a monk" said Ethelbald, "I would learn to read. But I am a prince, and it is foolish for princes to waste their time with such things."

13. "But I should like to know the story which this book tells," said Alfred.

14. A few weeks passed by. Then, one morning, Alfred went into his mother's room with a smiling, joyous face.

15. "Mother," he said, "will you let me see that beautiful book again?"

16. His mother unlocked her cabinet and took the fragile book from its place of safekeeping.

17. Alfred opened it with careful fingers. Then he began with the first word on the first page and read the first story aloud without making one mistake.

18. "O my child, how did you learn to do that?" cried his mother.

19. "I asked the monk, Brother Felix, to teach me," said Alfred. "And every day since you showed me the book, he has given me a lesson. It was no easy thing to learn these letters and how they are put together to make words. Now, Brother Felix says I can read almost as well as he."

20. "How wonderful!" said his mother.

21. "How foolish!" said Ethelbald.

22. "You will be a good monk when you grow up," said Ethelred, with a sneer.

23. But his mother kissed him and gave him the beautiful book. "The prize is yours, Alfred," she said. "I am sure that whether you grow up to be a monk or a king, you will be a wise and noble man."

24. And Alfred did grow up to become the wisest and noblest king that England ever had. In history he is called Alfred the Great.

If you don't know the answer, just guess! You will not be penalized for wrong answers, so you might as well give guessing a try!

Exercises

Re-read paragraph 1: "A thousand years ago boys and girls did not learn to read. Books were very scarce and very precious, and only a few men could read them."

1. What does the word **scarce** mean?

    A. Expensive
    B. Rare
    C. Easy to find
    D. Scary

2. Which best describes how the 3 older boys feel about the book?

    A. At first they think it's cool, but when they are told they have to learn to read, they think it's even cooler
    B. At first they think the book is uncool but after looking at the pictures they like it
    C. At first they think it's cool, but when they are told they have to learn to read, they think reading is for lower class people and no longer like the book
    D. They think the book is only for kings and princes.

3. Which best describes Alfred?

    A. He is the strongest of all the brothers
    B. He is determined and not bothered by the opinions of others
    C. He is easily persuaded by his older brothers
    D. His older brothers look up to him

Re-read paragraph 22: "You will be a good monk when you grow up," said Ethelred, with a sneer.

4. What is the author trying to tell you when he writes this?

    A. Ethelred thinks Alfred will actually be a great monk when he is older
    B. Ethelred is jealous of Alfred because he learned to read
    C. Ethelred thinks Alfred is foolish for wasting his time learning to read, and will have a worse job because of it
    D. Ethelred is a monk

5. Which statement best shows the theme of the passage?

    A. Be a good role model for your younger brothers
    B. Don't do any work that is below you
    C. Be kind to strangers
    D. Follow your dreams, no matter what people say

6. Which of the following statements would you include in a summary of the passage?

    A. Three young boys learn to read and tease their younger brother because he can't read yet.
    B. The youngest of 4 brothers learns to read despite his older brothers teasing him
    C. A mom teaches her young son to read
    D. 4 boys learn to read together

Why Indians Never Shoot Pigeons

1.   An Indian hunter went into the forest in search of food.
2.   The forest was so large that it would have taken three days to journey through it. All day he followed the track of the deer, but his arrows brought him no food.
3.   At night, he came to a dark, swift-running stream. He was tired and hungry.
4.   "Here," said he, "I will lie down and rest until sunrise."
5.   He began to search for a bed of pine needles, for the Indian loves the pine tree. It is his friend by day and by night. By day it is his forest guide. At night it gives him a soft, sweet-smelling bed on which to sleep, and it shields him from the storm.
6.   The hunter ran along the stream. It was very dark. He felt no soft pine needles under his feet, only the knotted roots of trees.
7.   Suddenly the great roots of an oak tree reached out and caught him. He could not free his foot from the oak's grasp.
8.   The sun rose and set. The great tree still held the hunter fast. He was weak from pain and hunger.
9.   It was now two days since he had tasted food. Four notches had been cut in his stick, for the Indian measures time in this way. Each sunrise and sunset, when he is on the trail, is marked by a notch on a small stick which he carries.
10.   Three times did the sun again rise and set, yet the tree did not let go its hold. There were now ten notches on the stick, and the hunter was so weak that he could scarcely cut the last one.
11.   As the sun rose on the fifth day, a bird flew into the tree. He saw the hunter lying on the ground, and came close and spoke to him.
12.   The hunter understood, for in those days men and birds could talk together.
13.   The bird asked the man what he could do for him, and the hunter whispered, "You are strong. You can fly a long trail. Go and tell the chief of my people."
14.   The bird flew swiftly away with the message. He did not wait until the sun was high. He did not stop to eat one berry or one worm. He did not fly high, nor fly low to talk with other birds. He went straight to the people the hunter had told him of.
15.   The West Wind tried to blow him back. A black cloud came up to frighten him, but he went through it. On, and on, and on, he went. Straight to the wigwam of the chief, he carried his message.
16.   The chief had called together the young men who were fast on foot, and was about to send them forth to find the lost hunter. They were asking the chief what trails they had best take. Before the chief could reply, a beautiful dove colored bird had flown close to his ear and had spoken to him in soft, low tones.
17.   The chief told the young men what the bird had said, and they set off on the trail the bird had named. Before sunset, they had found the lost hunter.
18.   Carefully they freed him from the grasp of the great oak and brought him back to his people. That night there was a feast and a dance in his honor.
19.   Ever since, the Indians have loved the birds that carry the messages, and they never shoot a pigeon.

Try answering multiple choice questions in your own words. See which answer choice best matches your answer.

Exercises

1. Which of the following is not a reason the Indian loves the pine tree?

  A. It keeps him safe from storms
  B. It gives him a soft bed to sleep in
  C. It helps give him food
  D. It helps guide him in the forest

2. Which best describes the notches on the stick?

  A. 1 notch for each full day
  B. 1 notch for each sunrise and 2 notches for each sunset
  C. 2 notches for each full day
  D. A notch represents each meal he has not eaten

Re-read these sentences from paragraph 14: "He did not wait until the sun was high. He did not stop to eat one berry or one worm. He did not fly high, nor fly low to talk with other birds."

3. What was the author trying to tell the reader about the bird?

  A. The bird had no friends to talk with
  B. He liked to fly in the dark
  C. He rushed as fast as he could to help the Indian
  D. He was not hungry when he flew

4. Which of the following best describes the bird?

  A. A brave bird looking for a reward
  B. A scared bird trying to prove he was brave
  C. A brave bird just trying to help out
  D. A bird who needed help so he helped the Indian first

5. What does paragraph 15 add to the story?

  A. It explains how the Indian got caught
  B. It shows why the bird helped the Indian
  C. It shows some of the troubles the bird had to face while helping the Indian
  D. It describes how the Indian thanked the bird

6. Which best describes the change from paragraph 10 to paragraph 14?

  A. At first the hunter is hopeful he will be rescued, but the bird takes too long
  B. At first the hunter is worried he won't be rescued, but the birds brave actions made the story seem more hopefully
  C. The bird changes from a friend to an enemy
  D. The bird changes from an enemy to a fiend

Find detailed video explanations to each problem on:
ArgoPrep.com

How Little Shooter Lost His Luck

1. One day, an Indian boy was playing beside a stream, when one of the little elf men came along in his canoe. The boy had his bow and arrow with him; so did the little elf man.

2. The little man stopped and offered to trade bows and arrows. The Indian boy looked first at his bow, and then at that of the little man. His bow was large. The little man's bow was very small. The boy thought his own bow was better, so he said he would not trade.

3. The little elf man laughed and drew his bow.

4. "You think only big things are great," he said. "Some day you will learn better. Some day you will want this little bow and these little arrows. Some day you will wish you had traded."

5. Then he shot an arrow into the clouds, sprang into his canoe, and paddled off up the stream. As he disappeared, he called back to the boy, "You will see me again, sometime!"

6. The Indian boy ran to his wigwam home. He told his father about the little man he had seen, and how the man wanted to trade bow and arrows.

7. "And you did not trade?" exclaimed the father.

8. "No," said the boy, "his bow was small; mine is large."

9. "Foolish boy!" said the father. "That little man was a Jo gah oh, one of the Little People. They do wonderful things. Their arrows are winged with power. Had you traded bows, you would have become a great hunter, and been able to get near the animals.

10. "Those little arrows of the Jo gah oh fly swift and far, and always bring back food. The boy who has a Jo gah oh bow and arrow always has good luck. One arrow of theirs is worth a ton of yours. Had you traded bow and arrows, you would have been called 'He shoots the sky.' Now you shall be called 'Little Shooter.'"

11. Little Shooter grew to be a man. He went often on the chase, but his arrows did not bring much game.

12. Many times, he wished he could meet the little elf man again, and trade bow and arrows, for sometimes he ran for days and found no track of deer or rabbit. But the little elf man never came.

13. One day, when Little Shooter had grown to be quite an old man, he was walking in the woods. He stopped under a tree to rest. Several times he felt something fall on his head.

14. At last he looked up to see what it was.

15. There sat the little elf man, swinging on the tip of a branch, and throwing nuts and twigs at him. He looked just as he did when Little Shooter met him by the stream long before. He had not grown old or changed at all.

16. "How long have you been here?" asked Little Shooter.

17. "I have always been here," said the little man. "I have been in the world ever since the stones were soft."

18. Then he laughed, and asked, "Does Little Shooter now like big bow and arrows best, or has he learned that sometimes small things are great? Next time, he had better trade with the little man," and aiming another nut at Little Shooter's head, he disappeared in the tree trunk.

Even for questions that don't ask you to re-read certain parts of the text, you should always go back into the text to check for your answer. This will prove you have the correct answer choice.

Exercises

Re-read paragraphs 1 and 2.

1. What is most likely the reason the author started the passage this way?

   A. To show the setting
   B. To set the stage for the problem
   C. To introduce the characters
   D. To explain background information

2. Which best describes how the boy's father feels?

   A. He is happy he did not trade the bow
   B. He is upset he did not trade the bow
   C. He is scared of the little person
   D. He is happy the boy traded the bow

Re-read paragraph 11.

3. What does the word **game** mean as it is used in this sentence?

   A. A fun game played in the woods
   B. Food from hunting animals
   C. Skill
   D. Fast thinking

4. Which statement best shows the theme in this passage?

   A. Don't judge a book by its cover
   B. Treat others the way you want to be treated
   C. Be kind to others
   D. Don't be tricked by strangers

5. In the passage "How Little Shooter Lost His Luck" the young Indian boy decides not to trade bow and arrows with the little man. What are some of the effects of his decision? Be sure to use at least 2 details from the text to support your answer.

6. In the passage "How Little Shooter Lost His Luck" the little man's bow and arrow turns out to be better than the young Indian's bow and arrow. What makes the little man's bow and arrow better? Be sure to use 2 details from the text to support your answer.

WEEK 16

VIDEO
EXPLANATIONS

ARGOPREP.COM

The Spider and the Fly

1. "Will you walk into my parlor?" said the spider to the fly;
2. "'Tis the prettiest little parlor that ever you did spy.
3. The way into my parlor is up a winding stair,
4. And I have many curious things to show when you are there."
5. "Oh no, no," said the little fly; "to ask me is a shame,
6. For who goes up your winding stair will never come down again."
7. "I'm sure you must be weary, dear, with soaring up so high.
8. Will you rest upon my little bed?" said the spider to the fly.
9. "There are pretty curtains drawn around; the sheets are fine and thin,
10. And if you like to rest a while, I'll snugly tuck you in!"
11. "Oh no, no," said the little fly, "for I've often heard it said,
12. They never, never wake again those who sleep upon your bed!"
13. Said the cunning spider to the fly: "Dear friend, what can I do
14. To prove the warm kindness I've always felt for you?
15. I have within my pantry good food of all that's nice;
16. I'm sure you're very welcome—will you please to take a slice?"
17. "Oh no, no," said the little fly; "kind sir, that cannot be:
18. I've heard what's in your pantry, and I do not wish to see!"
19. "Sweet creature!" said the spider, "you're witty and you're wise;
20. How handsome are your little wings; how brilliant are your eyes!
21. I have a little looking-glass upon my parlor shelf;
22. If you'll step in one moment, dear, you shall behold yourself."
23. "I thank you, gentle sir," she said, "for what you've had to say,
24. And, bidding you good morning now, I'll call another day."
25. The spider turned him round about, and went into his den,
26. For well he knew the silly fly would soon come back again:
27. So he wove a subtle web in a little corner sly,
28. And set his table ready to dine upon the fly;
29. Then came out to his door again, and merrily did sing:
30. "Come here, hither, pretty fly, with pearl and silver wing;
31. Your robes are green and purple; there's a crest upon your head;
32. Your eyes are like the diamond bright, but mine are dull as lead!"
33. Alas, alas! how very soon this silly little fly,
34. Hearing his kind, flattering words, came slowly flitting by;
35. With buzzing wings she hung aloft, then near and nearer drew,
36. Thinking only of her brilliant eyes and green and purple hue,
37. Thinking only of her crested head. Poor, foolish thing! at last
38. Up jumped the cunning spider, and fiercely held her fast;
39. He dragged her up his winding stair, into the dismal den—

Try thinking about the theme of the poem as you are reading. Make notes of what you think will happen or what the theme is to help you answer questions later on.

40.   Within his little parlor—but she never came out again!
41.   And now, dear little children, who may this story read,
42.   Don't let silly, flattering words give you a big head!
43.   And an evil creature will close their heart, ear and eye,
44.   So take a lesson from this tale of the spider and the fly.

Exercises

Re-read line 7.

1. What does the word **weary** mean?

  A. Happy
  B. Stupid
  C. Tired
  D. Smart

2. Which best describes the spider's goal in this poem?

  A. To become friends with the fly by inviting him into his home
  B. To eat the fly by tricking him with kindness
  C. To help the fly see that others might trick him
  D. To show the fly how he can trick others

3. Which best describes how the spider got the fly into his home?

  A. The fly wanted the food the spider offered him
  B. The fly liked the way the spider's home looked
  C. The fly liked all the compliments the spider was giving him
  D. The spider told him to come in for gifts and to sleep

4. Which best describes the fly?

  A. Someone who is easily flattered
  B. Someone who is caring
  C. Someone that likes to help others
  D. Someone who is tricked right away

Re-read line 27.

5. What does the author mean by this?

  A. The spider made a big web out in the open for the fly to see
  B. The spider made a small web out in the open for the fly to see
  C. Sneakily the spider made a small web
  D. Happily the spider made a small web

6. Which detail best shows the theme of the poem?

  A. Don't let silly, flattering words give you a big head!
  B. "I thank you, gentle sir," she said, "for what you've had to say,"
  C. So take a lesson from this tale of the spider and the fly.
  D. "Sweet creature!" said the spider, "you're witty and you're wise;

Hasty Charlie

1. Charlie never could wait. It was no use telling him "more calm, less speed," "slow and sure," or anything of that kind. You might as well talk to the walls. He got up in the morning, rushed over his routine that he was trusted to do for himself, hurried over his breakfast, rushed through his lessons, with many mistakes of course, and by his hasty, impatient behavior worried his quiet, gentle little sister Ethel nearly out of her wits, and almost drove patient Miss Smith, their homeschool teacher, to despair. He burnt his mouth with hot food, because he couldn't wait for it to cool; fell down-stairs, racing down, his toys were always getting broken because he couldn't stop to put them away; his bird flew away because he, fuming with impatience about something, forgot to fasten the cage door one day; Charlie was an impatient boy.

2. There were some exceptions to this general state of things. He didn't hurry to begin his lessons,—nor to go to bed. Here he would wait as long as you let him. One thing he had to wait for, against his will, was to grow up. It did take such a long time, and oh, the things he meant to do when once he was a man! Father hoped he would change a great deal before that time came, for, as he told him, a hasty, impatient man makes other people unhappy and cannot be happy himself.

3. Charlie meant to have a balloon when he grew up, and a sweet-stuff shop, an elephant, a garden full of apples and plums, a tall black horse, and a donkey.

4. "You needn't wait so long for the donkey," Father said one day. "I have seen a boy with two nice donkeys in Pine-tree Walk; when you and Ethel have been good children at your lessons, Miss Smith shall let you ride them, and when you can ride nicely I will buy you each a donkey of your own."

5. Lessons certainly went better after this, and the rides were much enjoyed on every fine day, though timid little Ethel was always just a wee bit afraid at first starting. Miss Smith always safely mounted Ethel first.

6. "Wait a minute, Charlie!" she said one day, when he was pulling and tugging impatiently at Neddie's leash, "we'll have you up on your donkey in just a minute."

7. But Charlie couldn't wait: he dragged the donkey into the road and jumped upon its back.

8. "Charlie! Charlie! you mustn't start without us. Wait a minute!"

9. "I can ride by my own self now," he said; and jerking the leash, off he went clattering down the road, the donkey-boy after him.

10. To mount a donkey is one thing, to control him is another, especially if you don't know how. On galloped Neddie, and after having knocked down a little girl and a barrow of fruit, he threw Charlie over his head, and having thus got rid of his rider began to enjoy himself on the grass. Poor Charlie! He had such a bruised face that he had to stay at home for days.

11. Miss Smith couldn't take him out like that. It hurt him very much, but it hurt him more when Father said that such a silly, impatient boy was not fit to be trusted to ride, and that he must wait a whole year before he could be allowed to mount a donkey again. "For your own sake, Charlie, and for other people's."

12. The little girl he had knocked down was more frightened than hurt; but Charlie was very sorry, for he was not at all a bad boy; and when he was at home by himself, while Ethel went for her donkey-rides, he had plenty of time to think things over, and made a good use of it.

Read each question carefully. You don't want to be tricked by a "not or does not." Check your work by re-reading the question and answer to make sure it makes sense.

13. At first he found it very hard to be patient, but after a little while he found it becoming much easier to wait, and every time he tried it became easier still.
14. Next summer, when Father gave him and Ethel the promised donkeys, he said, "I am proud to trust you now, Charlie, and hope that you will have some happy times with your donkey."
15. And very happy times they had.

Exercises

1. What does the word **hasty** mean?

A. Quick thoughtless movements or actions
B. Slow and well thought out actions
C. Quick but thoughtful actions
D. Slow and thoughtless actions

2. When wasn't Charlie quick and impatient?

A. When he was getting ready in the morning
B. Waiting for lessons at school
C. Waiting to ride the donkey
D. Waiting to grow up

3. Which best describes why Charlie tried to become more patient?

A. His father told him he would be in trouble until he became more patient
B. He didn't want his sister to be the only one with a donkey
C. He truly learned a lesson after running over the girl
D. Charlie needed to be more patient so that he could grow up faster

4. Which best describes Charlie's father?

A. Wise
B. Hasty
C. Slow
D. Stupid

5. How is paragraph 13 related to paragraph 14?

A. Paragraph 13 shows Charlie getting rewarded and paragraph 14 shows why he got this reward
B. Paragraph 13 explains why Charlie is impatient and paragraph 14 gives examples of times when he is impatient
C. Paragraph 13 gives details about Charlie's donkey and paragraph 14 gives details about Charlie
D. Paragraph 13 shows Charlie working toward becoming more patient and paragraph 14 shows his reward for being more patient.

6. Which statement belongs in a summary of this passage?

A. Charlie learns a lesson to finish his work quickly
B. Charlie learns how to ride a donkey
C. Charlie learns how to have patience
D. Charlie is a helpful kid

 ARGOPREP

Find detailed video explanations to each problem on:
ArgoPrep.com

Be Just Before You Are Generous

1. "Come, Kathie! It is time to go home!"

2. It was Mother who called: she had been sitting for the last hour under the shade of the old pier, while little Kathie ran around on the beach, sometimes paddling a little, sometimes building sand castles.

3. "Come, Kathie!" Mother called again; "it is late; come here and I will put on your shoes and socks."

4. Still Kathie did not move, but sat staring at the sea, but with a look in her eyes which told easily enough that her thoughts were far away. She was a a good, obedient child, but today she seemed almost as if she was afraid to come. Mother got up from her seat, and went towards the little one.

5. "Did you not hear me, Kathie?" she began; then in a different voice, "But, my child, where is your hat? Put it on at once, the sun is so hot."

6. Kathie hung her head, then the tears gathered in her eyes, and at last rolled quickly down her cheeks. "I haven't got a hat," she sobbed. "I gave it away. Are you vexed, Mother?"

7. Mother was puzzled. She sat down by Kathie and took her on her lap. "Don't cry," she said gently, "but tell me to whom you gave it."

8. "It was to a poor woman," said Kathie; "she asked me for it for her little girl, and so I took it off and gave it to her, but afterwards—"

9. "Afterwards you remembered that you should have asked Mother first," said Mother in an upset tone.

10. "Yes," said Kathie. "But, Mother, the woman was poor; we ought to give to the poor, ought we not?"

11. "Yes, Kathie, but we must only give that which is our very own. Now, the hat was not yours to give away; I bought it for you, to shade you from the hot sun."

12. "Oh, Mother!" interrupted Kathie, "then I can never give to the poor, for little children have nothing of their own." Kathie's lip shook, and she was very near crying at this thought.

13. "I will tell you what is your own to give," said Mother trying to cheer her, "that is your time. All children have a great deal of time to do as they like, and I can show you how you can use that time for the poor."

14. "Oh, mother! How? I can't sew nearly well enough to make anything for them."

15. "No, I don't mean sewing. I will give you an old pillow-case, and you must fill it with very little bits of torn, not cut, paper, and when it is full I will cover it for you with a case of pretty print, and then it will make a soft pillow for old Mrs. Timms, or anyone else you like to give it to. It will take both time and patience to tear the paper; and when it is finished it will be your own work, and you may give it away."

16. "Yes, I see," said Kathie. "That will be my own work. I shall like that."

17. "As you grow older you will have money and other things which you can give away, but even then you will find that your best gifts will be those you have spent time and love with; those two things are something even the of the poorest of us have, and yet they are worth more than gold and silver. Now, Kathie, we must go and buy you a new hat, for you cannot walk home in this heat without one; and another time when you give away anything you must remember to be just before you are generous."

18. Kathie thought Mother very kind not to be vexed about the hat; but Mother remembered what a little girl Kathie was, and she hardly expected her to be able to refuse, when a poor, old woman asked for the hat off her head.

 TIP of the DAY

When answering short response questions be clear about exactly how your details support your response. A simple sentence that starts with "This shows me that...." can help clarify why you used a certain detail.

Exercises

1. Why was Kathie staring out at the sea?

   A. She loved to watch the waves
   B. She wanted to build another sandcastle
   C. She was thinking about the hat she had just given away
   D. She was pretending not to hear her mother

3. Which best describes why Kathie shouldn't have given the hat away?

   A. Because her mother loved hats
   B. Because it was an expensive hat
   C. Because it was a gift from her mother
   D. All girls need hats

Re-read this sentence from paragraph 6: "I gave it away. Are you vexed, Mother?"

2. What does the word **vexed** mean in this sentence?

   A. Proud
   B. Happy
   C. Angry
   D. Cheerful

4. What kind of person is Kathie?

   A. Someone who is young and makes mistakes, but has a big heart
   B. Someone who is young and foolish
   C. A wise young girl who never makes mistakes
   D. An angry girl looking to get back at her mother

5. In the passage "Be Just Before You Are Generous" Kathie gives her hat away when she shouldn't have. Why shouldn't she have given her hat away? Give 2 reasons. Be sure to include details from the text to support your answer.

6. In the passage "Be Just Before You Are Generous" Kathie's mom plays an important role in this story. What kind of person is she? Be sure to use 2 details from the text to support your answer.

WEEK 17

VIDEO
EXPLANATIONS

ARGOPREP.COM

The Tinker's Van

1. "Ronald! Ronald! our van has come! John saw it go past the gate while we were in school."
2. "Has it!" exclaimed Fred Norton, no less excited at the news than his brother; "then let's go down at once and have a look at it."
3. Off ran the two little boys, and were soon in the village; and there, sure enough, stopped on a side street, was the van of a travelling tinker. The old horse had been taken out of the holder and was standing patiently on one side, while the tinker's wife, with her baby in her arms, walked slowly up and down, giving from time to time an anxious look up the street.
4. Her sunburnt face beamed with a hearty smile as the two boys rushed up to her.
5. "Here you are, young gentlemen!" she said, with evident delight; "I was looking out for you. I thought you'd see us go by; but my old man, he says, 'Susan, what are you thinking of? Those young gentlemen have forgotten you by this time, for it's six months more or less since we last passed by here.'"
6. "We haven't forgotten you," said little Ronald proudly. "How could I forget when you were so kind to me? I could not have got home that day I sprained my foot, and then your van came up, and you jumped out and carried me in, and bathed my foot, and brought me home. Why—why—" stammered the little fellow in his happiness, "I should be a pig if I forgot you."
7. "Step inside, sirs," said the woman, quite honored by Ronald's memory; "I want you to see how beautiful the clock looks that your mamma gave me. It goes just splendid; my old man is proud of it; it never loses a minute, and yet it gets many a jolt."
8. The children needed no second invitation. The van was a paradise to them, and they ran up the steps and looked at everything, and everything seemed amazing. They longed to have such a van, and thought the tinker and his wife must be the happiest of people.
9. "I should like to live here always," said Fred, as he and Ronald stood at the door of the van and looked out at the scene around them. "It's so jolly free," continued the boy, "so far better than always being in one house;—I'd much rather look at the things you see that at the maps and pictures on our schoolroom walls."
10. "Ah! but you don't know all, sir," said the woman, shaking her head. "I was born in a van, and have always lived in one, but I don't want my little baby here to lead this life," and she danced the swung the baby in her arms as she spoke. "I hope, by and by, we shall have a little cottage of our own and settle down, and my boy can go to school and learn to read, which is more than his mother can do, for I never had a day's schooling in my life."
11. "Can't you read?" said little Ronald in astonishment. "I'll come every day that you stay here and teach you. I'll begin tonight!" and before another word could be said he had darted out of the van and was up the street and out of sight, returning in a very few minutes with a large picture-book, out of which he himself had learned to read.
12. Ronald was a wise little fellow to have brought a picture-book; for such a work of art had never been seen by the woman before, and if reading was only looking at pictures like that she felt she be able to do it after all.
13. She was by no means a stupid scholar, and Ronald was so good of a little teacher that the progress made was really amazing. The tinker found a good many jobs in the village, working on everything

Finished early? Go back and make sure that you have answered all questions and that all of your answers make sense.

from fixing broken watches and bikes to making forks and knives. So she stayed nearly two weeks, and by that time Susan could spell little words very nicely, and no longer misread many words.

14. Ronald's mother gave the woman a large print book with a great many pictures in it; and when next year the tinker's van again visited the village, Susan was so excited to show off her progress, and slowly and proudly she read the story of the Little Red Riding Hood.

15. "I read that to my little boy most nights," she said; "he loves to listen to me read. Oh, Master Ronald!" said the woman, suddenly changing her tone, "I do thank you so much for putting it into my head to learn to read."

16. Certainly Ronald was a happy boy that day.

Exercises

1. What is a tinker?

A. Someone who makes and fixes things
B. A doctor
C. A lawyer
D. A magic healer

2. Which best describes why Ronald never forgot the woman?

A. Because she was beautiful
B. Because she had taken care of him when he hurt his foot
C. Because she was rich and had an amazing van
D. Because she was a tinker

3. What do Ronald and the woman have in common?

A. They are both parents
B. They both help each other and are grateful
C. They are from the same town
D. The are both tinkers

4. What changes from paragraph 11 to paragraph 15?

A. The woman forgets about the boy
B. The boy leaves town for a year
C. The woman learns to read
D. The boy learns to read

5. What does the woman tell the boys about living in a van?

A. It's great and everyone should do it
B. She tells them that she wishes she could live in a house and settle down
C. She offers to sell the van to the boys
D. She wants to raise her child in the van

6. Which could be included in a summary of this passage?

A. A tinker helps fix a boy's broken van
B. A woman and a boy are very kind to each other and are grateful for each other's help
C. A woman and a boy do each other favors in exchange for other favors
D. A tinker and a boy help each other out

The Colonial Peoples

1. In the beginning and in leadership the thirteen colonies, except New York and Delaware, were English. During the early days of all, besides these two, almost all of the immigration of people was from England. The colonists came from every walk of life. They were men, women, and children of "all sorts and conditions."

2. The major portion were small land owners, farm laborers, and artisans. With them were merchants and gentlemen who brought their stocks of goods or their fortunes to the New World. Scholars came from Oxford and Cambridge to preach the gospel or to teach. Now and then the son of an English nobleman left his noble hall behind and cast his chances with America. The people were from every religious faith.

3. New England was almost all English. During the years between 1629 and 1640, about twenty thousand people immigrated to America from England, settling in the colonies of the far North. Virginia, too, for a long time got almost all her immigrants from England alone. Not until right before the Revolution did other people, mainly the Scotch-Irish and Germans, come close to the English in numbers.

4. The populations of English colonies that formed later—the Carolinas, New York, Pennsylvania, and Georgia—still had a steady stream of immigration from England, but were constantly populated by people from the other places.

5. Next to the English in numbers and influence were the Scotch-Irish, Both religious and economic reasons sent them across the sea. Although no exact record was kept, it is thought that the Scotch-Irish and the Scotch who came directly from Scotland, composed one-sixth of the entire American population on the eve of the Revolution.

6. These newcomers in America made their homes mostly in New Jersey, Pennsylvania, Maryland, Virginia, and the Carolinas. Coming late upon the scene, they found much of the land right upon the shore already taken up. For this reason most of them became country people settling the inside and upland regions. There they cleared the land, laid out their small farms, and worked as hardy as they could.

7. Third among the colonists in order of numerical importance were the Germans. From the very beginning, they are shown in colonial records. A number of the artisans and carpenters in the first Jamestown colony were of German descent. Peter Minuit, the famous governor of New Motherland, was a German.

8. The large move of Germans began with the founding of Pennsylvania. Penn was smart in searching for useful farmers to cultivate his lands and he made a special effort to attract poorer people from the German country. A great company, known as the Frankfort Company, bought more than twenty thousand acres from him and in 1684 established a center at Germantown for the spreading out of German immigrants. In old New York, there was a similar center for spreading out the German people.

9. All the way from Maine to Georgia money was offered to the German farmers and in nearly every colony there were to be found, in time, German owned farms. In fact the migration became so large that German princes were frightened at the loss of so many subjects and England was alarmed by the rush of other people into her oversea lands. Yet nothing could stop the movement. By the end of the colonial period, the number of Germans had risen to more than two hundred thousand.

Keep track of important dates on the notes page. Write why each date was important so finding this information later will be much easier.

10. Wars, religious freedom, oppression, and poverty drove them all to America. Though most of them were farmers, there were also among them skilled artisans who helped with the rapid growth of industries in Pennsylvania. Their iron, glass, paper, and woolen mills, spread around here and there among the largely settled German regions, added to the wealth and independence of the soon to be state known as Pennsylvania.

11. Unlike the Scotch-Irish, the Germans did not speak the language of the original colonists or hang out freely with them. They kept to themselves, built their own schools, founded their own newspapers, and published their own books. Their independent habits often angered their neighbors and led to occasional fights against each other. However, no serious battles seem to have happened.

12. In the days of the Revolution, German soldiers from Pennsylvania fought in the patriot armies side by side with soldiers from the English and Scotch-Irish sections.

Exercises

Re-read this sentence from paragraph 1: "They were men, women, and children of "all sorts and conditions."

1. What does the author mean?

   A. Some people were sick and others weren't
   B. They were all the same kind of people
   C. There was all different kinds of people
   D. Man, woman or child everyone was sick

2. What does the word **immigrated** mean?

   A. Came here from another country to live
   B. Was forced to move to another country
   C. Like their own country best
   D. Wanted to move but couldn't

Re-read paragraph 3.

3. About how many people immigrated from England to the colonies from 1629-1640?

   A. 1,629
   B. 600
   C. 6,000
   D. 20,000

4. Which could be a reason the Germans separated themselves from the other colonists?

   A. They were a mean people
   B. They didn't want to make new friends
   C. They didn't speak the same language as the English and the Scotch-Irish people
   D. They had secrets they were keeping

5. Which best describes how the author organized this passage?

   A. In time order
   B. In order from his favorite country to his least favorite country
   C. The country with the most people to move to the colonies was first and the country with the least number of people to move to the colonies was last
   D. The country with the least number of people to move to the colonies was first and the country with the most number of people to move to the colonies was last

The Boyhood of Daniel Webster

1. Daniel Webster, the great statesman, speaker, and lawyer, was born on the 18th of January, 1782.

2. His father lived near the Merrimac River, and the only school within reach was a poor one kept open for a few months every winter. There Webster learned all that the country schoolmaster could teach him, which was very little; but he gained a hobby which did more for him than the reading, writing, and math of the school. He learned to like books, and to want knowledge; and when a boy gets really hungry and thirsty for knowledge it is not easy to keep him down. When some of the neighbors joined in setting up a little library, young Webster read every book in it two or three times, and even memorized a large part of the best of them. It was this eagerness for education on his part that led his father to send him to Dartmouth College.

3. There are not many boys in our time who could have spoke parts of Webster's great speeches; and it will interest them to know that the boy who made those speeches could never speak at all while he was at school. He learned his pieces well, and practiced them in his own room, but he could not speak them before people to save his life.

4. Webster was always fond of shooting and fishing, and, however hard he studied, the people around him called him lazy and idle, because he would spend whole days in these sports. Once, while he was studying under Dr. Woods to prepare for college, that gentleman spoke to him on the subject, and hurt his feelings a little. The boy went to his room planned to have revenge, and this is the way he took to get it.

5. The usual Latin lesson from Dr. Woods was one hundred lines of text, but Webster spent the whole night over the book. The next morning before breakfast he went to Dr. Woods and read the whole lesson from memory. Then he said:

6. "Will you hear a few more lines, doctor?"

7. The teacher agreeing, Webster read on and on and on, while the breakfast grew cold. Still there was no sign of the boy's stopping, and the hungry doctor at last asked how much farther he was prepared to read.

8. "To the end of the twelfth book" answered the "idle" boy, in triumph.

9. After that, Webster did not give up his hunting and fishing, but he worked so hard at his lessons, and got on so fast, that there was no further complaint of his "idleness." He not only learned the lessons given to him, but more, every day, and besides this he read every good book he could lay his hands on, for he was not at all happy just to know only what could be found in the school-books.

10. Webster's father was poor and in debt, but finding how hard working his boy was for school, and seeing, too, that he had extreme smarts, he tried, as hard as he could to afford to send him to college. Young Daniel went to Dartmouth College.

11. Many stories have been told to show the character of young Dan. He was always loose with his money when he had any. His brother was careful but generous, especially to Dan, whom he greatly looked up to. On one day the boys went to a neighboring town on a holiday, each with a quarter in his pocket.

12. "Well, Dan," said the father on their return, "what did you do with your money?"

13. "Spent it," answered the boy.

  TIP of the DAY *When answering short response questions, even if it doesn't tell you how many details to use, a safe bet is to always use at least 2 details to support your answer.*

14. "And what did you do with yours, Zeke?"
15. "Lent it to Dan," was the answer. The fact was that Dan had spent both quarters.
16. Young Webster was very focused in his studies, and as we have seen, he was physically strong and active as his love for sport proved; but he could never deal with farm-work. One day his father wanted him to help him in cutting hay with a long tool but very soon the boy complained that the tool was not made to suit him.
17. After finishing his college course Webster began studying law, but having no money, and being unwilling to ask his father for further support, he went into Northern Maine, and taught school there for a time. While teaching he saved all of his salary. With this money, he went to Boston, studied law, and soon made a name for himself as a lawyer. The story of his life as a public man, in the senate, in the cabinet, and as a famous lawyer, is well known, and does not belong to this sketch of his boyhood.

Exercises

Re-read paragraph 2.

1. What is the main reason the author includes this information?

   A. To show that Daniel was a good athlete
   B. To explain how Daniel became famous
   C. To show how much he loved learning
   D. To show his relationship with his father

3. Which best describes why Daniel began teaching?

   A. He loved teaching young kids
   B. He wanted to share his knowledge with students
   C. He needed money to go back to school to study law
   D. He wanted to give his money away to his parents

2. Which was the most effective way Daniel showed he wasn't "idle?"

   A. He played many sports
   B. He memorized many lessons from books and showed his teacher
   C. He sometimes fished all day
   D. He loved laying around and relaxing

4. Which statement best describes Daniel?

   A. He was a lazy boy who learned to love school
   B. He always loved school and was very smart but liked sports too
   C. He loved school but was not good at first and had to work very hard
   D. He wanted to become a teacher

5. In the passage, "The Boyhood of Daniel Webster" Daniel's teacher thinks he is "idle." What does idle mean? How does Daniel prove he isn't idle? Be sure to use 2 details from the text to support your answer.

6. In the passage, "The Boyhood of Daniel Webster" Daniel is very motivated to learn. Describe times when Daniel shows he is motivated and explain what he is motivated to do. Be sure to use details from the text to support your answer.

WEEK 18

VIDEO
EXPLANATIONS

ARGOPREP.COM

Why the Swallow's Tail is Forked

1. This is the story of how the swallow's tail came to be forked.
2. One day the Great Spirit asked all the animals that he had made to come to home. Those that could fly came first: the robin, the bluebird, the owl, the butterfly, the wasp, and the firefly. Behind them came the chicken, fluttering its wings and trying hard to keep up. Then came the deer, the squirrel, the snake, the cat, and the rabbit. Last of all came the bear, the beaver, and the hedgehog. Everyone traveled as swiftly as he could, for each wished to hear the words of the Great Spirit.
3. "I have called you together," said the Great Spirit, "because I often hear you yell and complain. What do you wish me to do for you? How can I help you?"
4. "I do not like to hunt so long for my food," said the bear.
5. "I do not like to build nests," said the bluebird.
6. "I do not like to live in the water," said the beaver.
7. "And I do not like to live in a tree," said the squirrel.
8. At last man stood up before the Great Spirit and said, "O Great Father, the snake feasts upon my blood. Will you not give him some other food?"
9. "And why?" asked the Great Spirit.
10. "Because I am the first of all the creatures you have made," answered man proudly.
11. Then every animal in the Great Spirit's home was angry to hear the words of man. The squirrel chattered, the wasp buzzed, the owl hooted, and the snake hissed.
12. "Hush, be still," said the Great Spirit. "You are, man, the first of my creatures, but I am the father of all. Each one has his rights, and the snake must have his food.
13. Mosquito, you are a great traveler. Now fly away and find what creature's blood is best for the snake. Come back in a year and a day."
14. The animals right went to their homes. Some went to the river, some to the forest, and some to the fields, to wait for the day when they must meet at the home of the Great Spirit.
15. The mosquito traveled over the earth and stung every creature that he met to find whose blood was the best for the snake. On his way back to the home of the Great Spirit he looked up into the sky, and there was the swallow.
16. "Good-day, swallow," called the mosquito.
17. "I am glad to see you, my friend," sang the swallow. "Are you going to the home of the Great Spirit? And have you found out whose blood is best for the snake?"
18. "The blood of man," answered the mosquito.
19. The mosquito did not like man, but the swallow had always been his friend. "What can I do to help man?" he thought. "Oh, I know what I can do." Then he asked the mosquito, "Whose blood did you say?"
20. "Man's blood," said the mosquito; "that is best."
21. "This is best," said the swallow, and he tore out the mosquito's tongue!
22. The mosquito buzzed angrily and went quickly to the Great Spirit.
23. "All the animals are here," said the Great Spirit. "They are waiting to hear whose blood is best for the snake."
24. The mosquito tried to answer, "The blood of man," but he could not say a word. He could make no sound but "Kss-ksss-ksssss!"

The real test is timed. If your teacher is timing you today, preview the whole assignment before beginning so that you know how much work you have to complete and you can better pace yourself.

25. "What do you say?"
26. "Kss-ksss-ksssss!" buzzed the mosquito angrily.
27. All the creatures wondered. Then said the swallow:
28. "Great Father, the mosquito is timid and cannot answer you. I met him before we came, and he told me whose blood it was."
29. "Then let us know at once," said the Great Spirit.
30. "It is the blood of the frog," answered the swallow quickly. "Is it not so, friend mosquito?"
31. "Kss-ksss-ksssss!" hissed the angry mosquito.
32. "The snake shall have the frog's blood," said the Great Spirit. "Man shall be his food no longer."
33. Now the snake was angry with the swallow, for he did not like frog's blood.
34. As the swallow flew near him, he grabbed him by the tail and tore away a little of it. This is why the swallow's tail is forked, and it is why man always looks upon the swallow as his friend.

Exercises

1. Which best describes why the Great Spirit called all of the animals together?

A. To find out who's blood is best for man
B. All of the animals had been complaining and the Great Spirit wanted to hear them
C. The animals were angry with the Great Spirit so he called them to his house
D. He called them to his house to punish them for complaining

Re-read paragraph 10.

2. Why does man say this?

A. He feels he is the most important creature and shouldn't be eaten by the snake
B. He is the first so he gets to go first when complaining
C. He feels he is the most important creature so she should make all of the rules
D. He wants to go first when deciding what they will eat

3. What do we learn about the swallow in paragraph 19?

A. He is a liar
B. He hates the mosquito
C. He is a friend of man
D. He is brave

4. Which best describes why the swallow's tail is forked?

A. He was born that way
B. The mosquito ripped it off in anger
C. Man forked his tail as a thank you
D. The snake grabbed his tail and ripped it in half in anger

5. Which could be included in a summary of the passage?

A. The mosquito had to find new food for himself
B. The mosquito had to find new food for the snake
C. The snake and the swallow are good friends
D. The snake likes to eat the frog

Why the Parrot Repeats the Words of Men

1. In the olden times when the earth was young, all the birds knew the language of men and could talk with them. Everybody liked the parrot, because he always told things as they were, and they called him the bird that tells the truth.

2. This bird that always told the truth lived with a man who was a thief, and one night the man killed another man's ox and hid its flesh.

3. When the other man came to look for it in the morning, he asked the thief, "Have you seen my ox?"

4. "No, I have not seen it," said the man.

5. "Is that the truth?" the owner asked.

6. "Yes, it is. I have not seen the ox," repeated the man.

7. "Ask the parrot," said one of the villagers. "He always tells the truth."

8. "O bird of truth," they said to the parrot, "did this man kill an ox and hide its flesh?"

9. "Yes, he did," answered the parrot.

10. The thief knew well that the villagers would punish him the next day, if he could not make them think that the parrot did not always tell the truth.

11. "I have it," he said to himself at last. "I know what I can do."

12. When night came he put a great black jar over the parrot. Then he poured water upon the jar and struck it many times with a tough piece of wood. This he did half the night. Then he went to bed and was soon fast asleep.

13. In the morning the men came to punish him.

14. "How do you know that I killed the ox?" he asked.

15. "Because the bird of truth says that you did," they answered.

16. "The bird of truth!" he cried. "That parrot is no bird of truth. He will not tell the truth even about what happened last night. Ask him if the moon was shining."

17. "Did the moon shine last night?" the men asked.

18. "No," answered the parrot. "There was no moon, for the rain fell, and there was a great storm in the heavens. I heard the thunder half the night."

19. "This bird has always told the truth before," said the villagers, "but there was no storm last night and the moon was bright. What shall we do to punish the parrot?" they asked the thief.

20. "I think we will no longer let him live in our homes," answered the thief.

21. "Yes," said the others, "he must fly away to the forest, and even when there is a storm, he can no longer come to our homes, because we know now that he is a bird of a lying tongue."

22. So the parrot flew away sorrowfully into the lonely forest. He met a mockingbird and told him what had happened.

23. "Why did you not repeat men's words as I do?" asked the mocking-bird. "Men always think their own words are good."

24. "But the man's words were not true," said the parrot.

25. "That is nothing," replied the mocking-bird, laughing. "Say what they say, and they will think you are a wonderful bird."

26. "Yes, I see," said the parrot thoughtfully, "and I will never again be punished for telling the truth. I will only repeat the words of others."

Be careful of tricky phrases such as main reason, in multiple choice questions. There may be more than one reason a character does something, but the question is only looking for the main reason.

Exercises

1. How did the thief trick the parrot?

   A. He didn't trick him, he made him lie to the other men
   B. He fooled him into thinking it was a dark and stormy night by putting the jar on his head
   C. He tricked him into lying by promising him many things
   D. He made the parrot think there was a bright shining moon

Re-read paragraphs 23-25. Then read the sentence below: ""That is nothing," replied the mockingbird, laughing".

4. Which best describes what the mockingbird meant when he says this?

   A. It doesn't matter what the truth is, man just wants to hear what he has already said
   B. You should always tell the truth no matter the consequences
   C. Don't listen to man, he is not truthful
   D. There is nothing you can do about it

2. Which best describes why they made the parrot leave?

   A. The parrot was a liar and man wanted to punish him for it
   B. The parrot was tricked into lying by the thief and they punished the parrot for it
   C. Man was angry that the parrot wouldn't lie for him so he made him leave
   D. The villagers didn't like birds around town anymore

5. What is the main reason the parrot will stop telling the truth?

   A. He doesn't like telling the truth anymore
   B. He will only repeat man because telling the truth will get him in trouble
   C. He wants everyone to like him so he's just going to be funny
   D. People like when parrots lie

Re-read this sentence from paragraph 22: "So the parrot flew away sorrowfully into the lonely forest."

3. What does the word **sorrowfully** mean?

   A. Quickly
   B. Slowly
   C. Happily
   D. Sadly

6. Which statement best describes the mockingbird?

   A. An evil bird who wants everyone to lie
   B. A bird who is looking out for the parrot
   C. A bird who works for man
   D. A bird who wants to trick the parrot

Find detailed video explanations to each problem on:
ArgoPrep.com

The Polar Bear

1. There is a special kind of bear called the polar bear. He lives in a place far up North, where it is always very cold. The land is nearly covered with snow, and the water at the top of the sea is frozen. There are no berries or fruits there for the polar bear to eat; so he has to live on fish, and seal, which is a water animal. The way the bear catches the fish or the seal is this:

2. He makes a hole in the ice with his paws, so that he can reach the water below. Then he sits down very quietly by the edge of the hole, and waits for a fish or a seal to swim past the hole. Then the bear pounces on it very quickly with his paw or his jaws, and catches it.

3. If the ice is too thick for the bear to make a hole through it, he has to try another way. He comes right down to the part of the sea where some of the ice has broken off. There he chooses a place at the edge of the ice, close to the water; and he waits there for a fish or a seal to swim past. Then he pounces on it and catches it.

4. Now I shall tell you a few special things that the polar bear has.

5. His coat of hair is much thicker than the coat of any other bear. Why? Because he lives in a colder place than any other bear; so he needs a thicker coat. Also, he sometimes has to swim through the icy water to get to some floating field of ice, so that he can catch fish from it. Then, although his hair gets wet, he has a thick lining of fat inside his coat to keep him warm.

6. The next special thing about the polar bear is that his hair is all white—like the color of everything around him, which, as I have told you, is just snow and ice. So when the polar bear sits down very quietly on the snow and ice, nobody can see him even from a short distance, because he is the same color as the snow and ice. And that is why the fish or the seal does not see him, and so gets caught.

7. That is one of the wonderful things about many wild animals—they are of the same color as the place where they live. You know that the color of a lion is yellow, like the color of sand; and the lion lives in countries where there are lots of sandy places. You know, too, that the color of a tiger is yellow, but with black stripes upon the yellow, so that if you looked at him from a distance, you might think he was made up of yellow and black stripes. And the tiger lives in the tall grass, which also looks like yellow and black stripes.

8. But now I shall tell you more about the polar bear. He has three other special things: the soles of his feet are hairy; he has a small head; and he has a long neck.

9. First, about the soles of his feet. The soles of the feet of other bears are smooth, just like the feet of all other animals that have to walk on ordinary ground. But the soles of the polar bear are covered with long hair, just as is his body. Why? Because he has to walk on ice, which is very slippery, and he needs to have the soles of his feet covered with hair, or else he would slip on the ice, just as you must wear rubbers over your shoes when you have to walk on icy ground.

10. He has a smaller head than any other kind of bear. Why? To make it easier for him to put his head through the hole in the ice, when he is catching fish. Other kinds of bears do not have to put their heads into a hole to get anything to eat; so they do not need to have a small head.

11. The polar bear has also a longer neck than any other kind of bear. Why? To give him a longer reach in catching the fish with his jaws—without tumbling into the water himself. Other bears, who live on dry land, do not need to reach out like that, and so they have shorter necks.

TIP of the DAY

Adding headings to paragraphs or multiple paragraphs can help identify the main idea for sections of text. This can help you better understand the text and answer questions later on.

Exercises

Re-read paragraph 1.

1. Why does the author being the passage this way?

    A. To introduce himself to the reader
    B. To show a little bit of the setting and set up the information in the rest of the passage
    C. To describe how the polar bear hunts
    D. To describe parts of the polar bear's body

2. Which best describes how paragraph 2 is related to paragraph 3?

    A. Paragraph 2 shows what happens when the ice is too thick for the polar bear and paragraph 3 explains when the ice isn't too thick
    B. Paragraph 2 shows how the polar bear eats when the ice isn't too thick and paragraph 3 explains what happens when the ice is too thick
    C. Paragraph 2 and paragraph 3 are not related
    D. Paragraph 2 explains what the polar bear's feet look like and paragraph 3 shows how uses them

3. Why does the author include the information found in paragraph 7?

    A. To give more details about how polar bears camouflage themselves
    B. To explain how the polar bear uses his long neck
    C. To compare polar bears to other animals that camouflage themselves
    D. To trick the reader

4. Which would be a better title for this passage?

    A. How polar bears protect themselves from prey
    B. How polar bears use their bodies to survive
    C. When polar bears attack
    D. Polar bears are bad hunters

5. In the passage, "The Polar Bear" the author talks about many of the polar bear's traits that are good for hunting. What are 2 of the traits the polar bear has that are good for hunting and how do they help? Be sure to use details from the text to support your answer.

6. What is the main idea of the passage, "The Polar Bear?" Be sure to use 2 details from the text to support your answer.

WEEK 19

VIDEO
EXPLANATIONS

ARGOPREP.COM

The Virginia Wife-Market

1. The first English colony in America that came to be was made in the most absurd way possible. A great company of London merchants set about the work of putting an English colony in Virginia, and they were very eager about it too.

2. They knew that the colonists must have something to eat and must defend themselves against the Indians, and so it must have made sense to them that the first men sent out must be strong farmers, who could cut down trees, plough the ground, raise food enough for the people to eat, and handle guns well, if need be.

3. The work to be done was that of farmers, woodchoppers, and men who could make a living for themselves in a new country. Then, after those men had cleared some land, built some houses, and raised their first crop, men of other kinds might have been sent there.

4. But that was not the way in which the London Company went to work. They chose for their first settlers the most unfit men they could have found for such a purpose. There were one hundred and five of them in all, and forty-eight of them were what people in those days called "gentlemen"—that is to say, they were the sons of rich men.

5. They had never learned how to do any kind of work, and had been brought up to think that a gentleman could not work without lowering himself and losing his right to be called a gentleman. There were a good many "servants" also in the party, and probably most of them were brought to wait upon the gentlemen. There were very few farmers and not many mechanics in the party, although farmers and mechanics were the men most needed.

6. None of the men brought families with them. They were single men, who came out to this country, not to make comfortable homes for wives and children, but to find gold and pearls, or to grow rich in some other quick and easy way, and then to go back and live in ease in England.

7. Luckily, there was one man of sense and spirit among them—the celebrated Captain John Smith—who got them to work a little, and, after many hardships and two or three narrow escapes from failure, the colony was firmly in place.

8. The London Company sent out ships every year with supplies and new people; but, strange as it seems, most of the men that were sent were unmarried, and even those who had wives and children left them in England.

9. When we think of it, this was a very bad way to start a new country. The single men did not want to stay all their lives in a country where there were no women and children. They meant to make some money as quickly as they could and then go back to England to live. The married men who had left their families behind them were in still greater hurry to make money and go home. If the men would have come with wives and children in Virginia, they would have done all they could to make the new colony a good one to live in: they would have built good houses, set up schools, and worked hard to improve their own lives and to keep order in the colony.

10. Sir Edwin Sandys was the wise man who saw all this most clearly. He knew that if these single men were to stay in Virginia and become happy they must have a chance to marry and set up homes of their own. So he went to work in England to get together a cargo of sweethearts for the men. He persuaded ninety young women of good character to go out in one of the company's ships, to marry young men in Virginia.

Don't pay attention to patterns of answer choices. There is no pattern. There can be 10 C's in a row or no C's in the whole test. However neither is likely.

11. The plan was an odd one, but it was managed with good sense and did well for everybody involved. It was agreed that the company should provide the young women with such clothing and other things as they would need for the voyage, and should give them free passage on board the ship. When they landed in Virginia they were to be perfectly free to marry or not. If any of them did not at once find husbands to their liking they were to be cared for in good homes until they chose to marry.

12. It was an odd thing to do, of course, but the times were very unusual, and the plan of importing sweethearts by the cargo really seems to have been a very good one.

Exercises

1. Which kind of person was best fitted to come to start the colony at first?

A. A gentleman
B. A woman
C. A strong farmer
D. A teacher

2. Which kind of person actually came over the most at first?

A. Gentlemen
B. Women
C. Strong Farmers
D. Teachers

3. Which best describes why the men didn't bring their families?

A. They wanted to start new lives
B. They wanted to make money quick and then return home
C. Women were not allowed in the colonies
D. They thought the women wouldn't be any help

Re-read all of paragraph 10, then read this sentence: "So he went to work in England to get together a cargo of sweethearts for the men."

4. What does the author mean by a cargo of sweethearts for the men?

A. A ton of candy
B. Teddy Bears and Cards
C. Their wives from back home
D. Women whom they could marry

5. What happened to the women who didn't marry right away?

A. They were sent to jail
B. They were sent right back home to England
C. They were cared for until they found a husband they liked
D. They were forced to marry

6. Which best describes why it would have been better for the men to bring their wives and children to begin with?

A. So they could also work and make money
B. So the men would care more about the place they lived in and work harder for it
C. So they could have better cooking
D. So they could go home quicker

Charlie's Word

1. "Well, children, I'll let you go and have this picnic by yourselves if you'll give me your word that you'll behave just as you would do if I were with you. Will you promise?"

2. "Yes, Nurse, we do promise; and we'll keep our word," said Algy Parker, "won't we?" and he turned round to Charlie, Basil, and little Ivy, as if to ask them to confirm his words.

3. "Yes, we promise," they repeated, full of delight to think that they might actually picnic by themselves for a whole day.

4. "Don't leave the Home Fields, now," said Nurse. "You can't do too much harm there, I should think; and I should be happy for a free day, so I can get the gardens cleaned out before your mother comes tomorrow; so mind your promise, and take good care of little Miss Ivy."

5. In a very short time all was ready. Cook had packed a most tempting lunch of ham sandwiches, plum-cake, and gooseberry turnovers, and this was placed in a basket on Algy's bike; and then off he started, and Charlie and Basil, with little Ivy between them, ran after him down the long road, laughing and singing as joyfully as young birds.

6. The Home Fields were at the bottom of the road, and the children were no sooner in them than Ivy gave a scream of delight. "The roses, Algy! The wild roses are out; oh, do pick me some!"

7. Ivy always got her own way with her brothers; and Algy stopped, threw off his hat, pulled out his clasp-knife, and gathered a good bunch of the delicate blossoms for the little queen.

8. Charlie did not care for roses; he was better liked with the duck-pond, and began building a little bridge for himself with some stones that lay near, much to the unhappiness of a pair of old ducks, who thought the pond to be their private property, and very much hated Charlie's bridge.

9. "Just listen to old Mrs. Quack talking to me," cried Charlie, smiling to himself as he stood some little way in the pond. As he spoke, however, one of the stones of the bridge slipped, and Charlie stumbled right into the water!

10. Nurse strictly forbade wet boots, and Charlie well knew that had she been there he would at once be sent back to the house to change them, and might think himself lucky if he escaped being put to bed as a punishment.

11. Such things had happened before now in the Parker nursery; and Charlie remembered also there was no mother at home today to get him out of trouble, as she often had done. But for all that Charlie's mind was made up; he had given his word to behave as if Nurse were by, and so he must go home.

12. "Perhaps she'll put you to bed," sobbed little Ivy.

13. "I can't help it," said Charlie sorrowfully. "I must keep my word."

14. So the poor boy went back manfully back to the house to find his worst fears realized. Nurse was very busy and consequently angry; and on hearing Charlie's tale and seeing his boots, she sent him off to bed. "He'd be dry enough there," she muttered.

15. Charlie knew there was no help for it, Nurse would be listened to; so slowly and sorrowfully he began undressing, the large tears rolling down his cheeks, when the door opened and Mother stood there! She had come back sooner than was expected; and before Charlie could say anything she realized all that was happening. Nurse quickly helped him put on his dry boots, and Mother and he were walking quickly towards the Home Fields. How the children did scream with delight when they found that Mother herself was going to picnic with them.

Follow the directions of the question exactly. If it says what did we learn in paragraph 11, don't think about the character or text as a whole, focus on paragraph 11.

16.   "You must thank Charlie that I am here," said Mother. "If he had not kept his promise to Nurse I should not have known where to find you;" and Mother looked fondly at her honest little boy.

17.   "You see, I had to," said Charlie simply: "I had given my word."

Exercises

Re-read paragraph 1.

1. Why does the author start the passage this way?

   A. To show the setting
   B. To introduce the characters
   C. To tell what the promise is and the story will be about
   D. To give background on the main character

Re-read this phrase from paragraph 7: "Ivy always got her own way with her brothers"

2. Which detail best helps you understand what the author means by this?

   A. "The roses, Algy!"
   B. Charlie and Basil, with little Ivy between them
   C. Algy... gathered a good bunch of the delicate blossoms for the little queen.
   D. Nurse strictly forbade wet boots,

3. What do we learn about Charlie in paragraph 11?

   A. He got his boots wet
   B. He liked ducks better than roses
   C. He loved his mother
   D. He was going to be honest

Re-read this phrase from paragraph 15: "Nurse quickly helped him put on his dry boots"

4. Why do you think Nurse did this?

   A. She realized she was wrong all along to punish him
   B. Charlie's mother came home and Nurse was scared of getting in trouble for punishing the boy
   C. Nurse just wanted Charlie to have dry boots the whole time
   D. She only trying to teach Charlie a lesson

5. Which best describes something that happened because Charlie told the truth?

   A. His mother came home
   B. His mother went with him back to the Home Fields with his brothers and sister
   C. Nurse forgave Charlie
   D. Little Ivy came home too

6. Which best shows the theme of this passage?

   A. Always be on your best behavior
   B. Always tell the truth and good things will happen
   C. Treat your brothers and sisters nicely
   D. Listen to your parents

Find detailed video explanations to each problem on:
ArgoPrep.com

1. How The Iroquois Give Thanks

2. The Iroquois Red Children are a grateful people. The true Iroquois never rises after eating without saying, "Niaweh," which means, "I am thankful." The others reply, "Niuh,"—"It is well."

3. The Red Children never pick a flower without thinking how kind the Great Spirit has been, to cause the flowers to grow. They like flowers, and no matter how poor the Indian cabin, flowers are always to be found near.

4. When the Iroquois pick fruit, they give thanks to the Great Spirit. And always do they leave some, for the "little brothers of the wood."

5. They do not try to pick every cherry or berry, or nut or apple, for themselves. Fruits grow for the birds and animals as well as for men, and the little brothers of the wood must not be forgotten. Some of everything that grows is left for them.

6. During the spring and summer, the Iroquois give several thanksgiving feasts. The first is early in the spring, at maple-sugar time. As soon as the sap begins to flow, the Maple Feast is called.

7. The Indians gather about a large maple tree. A fire is lighted near, upon which one of their people sprinkles tobacco. As the smoke rises, a prayer of thanksgiving is made to the Great Spirit, for causing the sweet waters of the maple to flow. Then the maple trees are thanked for their service to men, and protection is asked for the trees during the coming year.

8. When "the leaf of the dogwood tree is the size of a squirrel's ear," it is planting time. Then an Indian maid goes into the fields and scatters a few grains of corn, asking the aid of the Great Spirit for the harvest. The Indian always plants his seed with the growing moon, that it may grow with the moon.

9. The next feast is the Strawberry Feast and Dance.

10. The strawberry is one of the best gifts of the Great Spirit to his children. So highly is it thought of that it is said to grow on the Sky Road that leads to the Heaven. An Indian who has been very ill, near death, will say, "I almost ate strawberries."

11. When the strawberry ripens, the Red Children are happy. They sing their praises to the Great Spirit and dance with joy. They remember the Little People who have helped to make the berries beautiful, and they have a song of praise and dance of thanks for them as well. Without the help of the Little People, the strawberries would not be so sweet and ripe.

12. At the time of the Harvest Moon comes the last feast of the summer. This thanksgiving feast lasts four days. The Indians not only give thanks for the ripening of the corn, but for every growing thing. Therefore this feast is longer than the others, since it takes some time to name all the good gifts of the Great Spirit to the Red Children, and to give thanks for them all.

13. There is a story of the corn in which the Spirit of the Corn is a woman, not a handsome young chief, as one of the stories claims. This Corn Spirit was one of three sisters, and was called Ona tah.

14. The three sister vegetables—the corn, the bean, and the squash—were called the Di o he ko, which means "those we live on," since they are the life-giving vegetables.

15. These sisters lived together on a hill and were very happy. But one day Ona tah wandered away in search of water for her seeds.

  *Be aware of distractor answers. These are answers that may appear right but are missing a key element or contain a single word that makes the answer choice incorrect. Be careful!*

16. The Evil Spirit was watching. He kidnapped Ona tah, the Spirit of the Corn, and sent one of his monsters to steal in her fields. The killing winds swept over the hill, and the spirits of the squash and bean fled before them

17. Ona tah was held for some time a prisoner in the darkness under the earth, by the Evil Spirit until her 2 sisters saved her.

Exercises

1. Which detail best helps you understand who the 'little brothers of the wood" were?

   A. They give thanks to the Great Spirit
   B. Some of everything that grows is left for them.
   C. Fruits grow for the birds and animals as well as for men
   D. "When the leaf of the dogwood tree is the size of a squirrel's ear"

3. Why did Ona tah leave the three sisters?

   A. She thought she was more important
   B. She wanted to find water for her seeds
   C. She knew the Evil Spirit was coming
   D. She was scared

2. What is the Corn Spirit's name?

   A. Spirit of the Corn
   B. Ona tah
   C. Three Sisters
   D. Di o he ko

4. How does the author organize this passage?

   A. In time order
   B. In order of her favorite festivals
   C. Each festival has its own section
   D. There is no order

5. In the passage "How The Iroquois Give Thanks" there are many feasts to give thanks. Name 2 of the feasts and why they are celebrated. Be sure to use details from the text to support your answer.

_____

_____

_____

_____

_____

_____

_____

_____

_____

_____

6. In the passage "How The Iroquois Give Thanks" there are many feasts to give thanks. Which feast seems to be the most important? Why? Be sure to use at least 2 details from the text to support your answer.

_____

_____

_____

_____

_____

_____

_____

_____

_____

_____

WEEK 20

VIDEO
EXPLANATIONS

ARGOPREP.COM

The Story of a Great Story

1. Two hundred years ago there lived a young man whose name was Alexander Selkirk. He lived in Scotland. He was often making trouble among his neighbors.

2. For this reason many people were glad when he ran away from home and went to sea. "We hope that he will get what he deserves," they said.

3. He was big and strong and soon became a fine sailor. But he was still stubborn and poorly behaved; and he was often in trouble with the other sailors.

4. Once his ship was sailing in the great Pacific Ocean. It was four hundred miles from the coast of South America. Then something happened which Selkirk did not like. He became very angry. He fought with the other sailors, and even with the captain.

5. "I would rather live alone on a desert island than be a sailor on this ship," he said.

6. "Very well," answered the captain. "We shall put you ashore on the first island that we see."

7. "Do so," said Selkirk. "You cannot please me better."

8. The very next day they came in sight of a little green island.

9. "Set me on shore and leave me there. Give me a few common tools and some food, and I will do well enough," said the sailor.

10. "It shall be done," answered the captain.

11. So they filled a small boat with the things that he would need the most—an ax, a knife, a kettle, and some other things. They also put in some bread and meat and other food, enough for several weeks.

12. Then four of the sailors rowed him to the shore and left him there.

13. Alexander Selkirk was all alone on the island. He began to see how foolish he had been; he thought how terrible it would be to live there without one friend, without one person to whom he could speak.

14. He called loudly to the sailors and to the captain. "Oh, do not leave me here. Take me back, and I will give you no more trouble."

15. But they would not listen to him. The ship sailed away and was soon lost to sight.

16. Then Selkirk set to work to make the best of things. He built himself a little hut for shelter at night and in stormy weather. He planted a small garden. There were pigs and goats on the island, and plenty of fish could be caught from the shore. So there was always plenty of food.

17. "If I ever have the good luck to escape from this island," he said, "I will be kind to everyone. I will try to make friends instead of enemies."

18. For four years and four months he lived alone on the island. Then, to his great joy, a ship came near and stopped in the little harbor.

19. He made himself seen, and the captain agreed to take him back to his own country. When he reached Scotland everybody was eager to hear him tell of his adventures, and he soon found himself famous.

20. In England there was then living a man whose name was Daniel Defoe. He was a writer of books.

21. When Daniel Defoe heard how Selkirk had lived alone on the island he said to himself: "Here is something worth telling about. The story of Alexander Selkirk is very pleasing."

22. So he sat down and wrote a wonderful story, which he called "The Adventures of Robinson Crusoe."

23. Every boy has heard of Robinson Crusoe. Many boys and many girls have read his story.

24. Robinson Crusoe sailed first on one ship and then on another. He visited many lands and saw many wonderful things.

Relax. Don't stress it's just a test. Whatever you have to say to stay calm. The more relaxed you are the faster and better your brain can work. Crush it!

25. One day there was a great storm. The ship was driven about by the winds; it was wrecked. All the sailors were drowned except Robinson Crusoe.

26. He swam to an island that was not far away. It was a small island, and there was no one living on it. But there were birds in the woods and some wild goats on the hills.

27. For a long time Robinson Crusoe was all alone. He had only a dog and some cats to keep him company. Then he tamed a parrot and some goats.

28. He built a house of some sticks and vines. He used grain and baked bread. He made a boat for himself. He did a great many things. He was busy every day.

29. At last a ship happened to pass that way and Robinson was taken on board. He was glad to go back to England to see his home and his friends once more.

30. This is the story which Mr. Defoe wrote. Perhaps he would not have thought of it, had he not first heard the true story of Alexander Selkirk.

Exercises

1. Which best describes how the story of Robinson Crusoe came to be?

   A. Selkirk wrote it himself after his adventures
   B. A writer came up with the idea that had nothing to do with Selkirk
   C. Selkirk helped a writer with the book
   D. A writer came up with the idea after being inspired by Selkirk's story

2. What changes between paragraph 5 and 13?

   A. First Selkirk likes the sailors, then he hates him
   B. First he thinks he would be better off alone, then he realizes he wants to be around people
   C. He turns from a boy into a man
   D. First he is on the island, then he escapes the island

3. Which best describes the main thing Alexander Selkirk learned while on the island?

   A. How to hunt and fish
   B. How to build a home
   C. Be kinder to everyone
   D. How to defend himself

4. How does the author organize this passage?

   A. In time order
   B. In order of important events
   C. First the real story was told then the story about the story was told
   D. First the story about the story was told, then the real story

Re-read paragraph 17.

5. Which best describes why Selkirk says this?

   A. He is angry about being left on the island
   B. He wishes he had brought more friends with him
   C. He realizes that he is only on the island because of his behavior and he wants to change
   D. He is saying that to trick the sailors into liking him

6. How long was Selkirk on the island for?

   A. 4 months
   B. 4 years
   C. 4 years and 4 months
   D. 20 years

Britain Before Written History Began - The Earliest People of England

1. England was inhabited for many many years before its written history began. The earliest people that lived the country were short, brutal savages. They used pieces of rough rock for tools and weapons. From rocks they also produced fire. They lived by hunting and fishing, and often had no homes but caves and rock shelters.

2. Following the Cavemen came a people that had learned how to grind and polish the stone of which they made their knives and spears. These people cleared and farmed the soil and kept cattle and other house animals.

The British

3. Finally, a light-haired, fierce-eyed people came and conquered the island. They came from the west of Europe. They made their axes, swords, and spears of bronze. These weapons were far superior to any made of stone.

4. The new people were good farmers; they sold grain, cattle, tin, and ore to merchants who came by sea from the east.

5. These strong and energetic people, known as Celts, eventually called themselves British. By the time they had changed that name they had made a great step forward, for they had learned how to mine and make iron—the most useful metal known to man; from it they made swords, and spears.

The Religion of the British

6. The British held a little faith in a God and in a life beyond the grave. They offered gifts to that God, and when they buried one of their warriors, they buried his spear with him so that he might fight as good a battle in the next world as he had fought in this one.

7. Also, the British had a class of priests called Druids, who seem to have worshiped the heavenly bodies. These priests also acted as judges and teachers. The Druids taught kids about the stars and their motions, about the power of the earth, the nature of things, and "the might and power of the immortal gods."

8. More than this, the Druids built the giant stone strange statues open to the sky, whose ruins may still be seen today on the lonely island of Salisbury Plain.

9. Stonehenge, as it would come to be know, is this amazing structure believed to be the remains of a prehistoric tribute to the dead, which was used also as a place of worship.

10. Here's what it looks like; a broken circle of huge upright stones, some of which are still connected at the top by blocks of flat stones. Within this circle, which is about one hundred feet around, is a circle of smaller stones. The structure has no roof. The recent discovery of bronze or copper on one of the great stones, seven feet below the surface, makes us believe in the theory that Stonehenge was constructed by the race who used bronze implements and who were later known as British.

What we owe to Prehistoric Man

11. To them we owe man's wonderful discovery of the power to produce fire. To them we are thankful for the invention of the first tools, the first weapons, and the first attempts at building house and art. They too tamed the dog, the horse, and our other domestic animals. They also discovered how to till the soil and how to mine and manufacture metals. In fact those who lived in "the childhood of the world," and who never wrote a line of history, did some things equal to anything in history.

Use the subheadings to help you understand the text better. Make notes next to each section or underline important information you can easily find later.

12. Finally, through their tiresome struggles with nature, and ongoing wars among themselves, these tribes learned to establish forms of self-government and towns. Many of their customs—their unwritten laws—still make themselves felt in the world. They help keep the English nation together. They do even more than that. Their influence can be found in the laws of newer nations, like America.

Exercises

Re-read paragraph 1.

1. According to paragraph 1, what didn't the early people use rocks for?

A. Art
B. Tools
C. Weapons
D. Fire

2. What do paragraphs 8-10 show about the Druids?

A. They were teachers
B. They were judges
C. They built an amazing structure called Stonehenge
D. They were good farmers

Re-read this phrase from paragraph 11: "the childhood of the world"

3. What does the author mean by this?

A. Everyone in England was a child
B. Everyone in England acted like a child
C. People who lived in the beginning of the world
D. People who moved to England after Stonehenge was built

4. How does the author describe prehistoric man?

A. Foolish and unwise
B. Very smart and influential
C. Bullies
D. Weak

5. Which best describes when this passage was most likely written?

A. Five years ago
B. A long time ago, but America had been a country for a long time
C. A long time ago when America first became a country
D. Yesterday

6. Which detail best helped you answer question number 5?

A. Their influence can be found in the laws of newer nations, like America
B. England was inhabited for many many years before its written history began
C. The new people were good farmers; they sold grain, cattle, tin, and ore to merchants who came by sea from the east
D. In fact those" who lived in "the childhood of the world," and who never wrote a line of history, did some things equal to anything in history.

Lazy Jack

1. Once upon a time there was a boy whose name was Jack, and he lived with his mother on a hill. They were very poor, and the old woman got her living by spinning, but Jack was so lazy that he would do nothing but bask in the sun in the hot weather, and sit by the corner of the fire in the wintertime. So they called him Lazy Jack. His mother could not get him to do anything for her, and at last told him, one Monday, that if he did not begin to work for his food at home she would kick him out to get his living as he could.

2. This motivated Jack, and he went out and got a job for himself for the next day to a nearby farmer for a penny; but as he was coming home, never having had any money before, he lost it in passing over a creek.

3. "You stupid boy," said his mother, "you should have put it in your pocket."

4. "I'll do so another time," replied Jack.

5. Well, the next day, Jack went out again and got himself a job as a cowkeeper, who gave him a jar of milk for his day's work. Jack took the jar and put it into the large pocket of his jacket, spilling it all, long before he got home.

6. "Dear me!" said the old woman; "you should have carried it on your head."

7. "I'll do so another time," said Jack.

8. So the following day, Jack got himself a job with a farmer, who agreed to give him a cream cheese for his services. In the evening Jack took the cheese, and went home with it on his head. By the time he got home the cheese was all spoiled, part of it being lost, and part stuck with his hair.

9. "You stupid boy," said his mother, "you should have carried it very carefully in your hands."

10. "I'll do so another time," replied Jack.

11. Now the next day, Lazy Jack again went out, and got himself a job with a baker, who would give him nothing for his work but a large tom-cat. Jack took the cat, and began carrying it very carefully in his hands, but in a short time large cat scratched him so much that he had to let it go.

12. When he got home, his mother said to him, "You silly fellow, you should have tied it with a string, and dragged it along after you."

13. "I'll do so another time," said Jack.

14. So on the following day, Jack got himself a job with a butcher, who rewarded him by the handsome present of a shoulder steak. Jack took the steak, tied it with a string, and trailed it along after him in the dirt, so that by the time he had got home the meat was completely ruined. His mother was this time quite out of patience with him, for the next day was Sunday, and she going to use the steak for her dinner.

15. "You ninney-hammer," said she to her son, "you should have carried it on your shoulder."

16. "I'll do so another time," replied Jack.

17. Well, on the Monday, Lazy Jack went once more and got himself a job with a cattlekeeper, who gave him a donkey for his trouble. Now though Jack was strong he found it hard to lift the donkey on his shoulders, but at last he did it, and began walking home slowly with his prize.

Look at each question for key words. When you read the text and see the key words you can have that "Ah-Ha" moment and know you've found a key to answering a question!

18. Now it so happened while on his walk home he passed a house where a rich man lived with his only daughter, a beautiful girl, who was deaf and couldn't speak. And she had never laughed in her life, and the doctors said she would never speak till somebody made her laugh.

19. So the father had said that any man who made her laugh would receive her hand in marriage. Now this young lady happened to be looking out of the window when Jack was passing by with the donkey on his shoulders; and the poor animal with its legs sticking up in the air was kicking violently and "heehawing" with all its might. Well, the sight was so ridiculous that she burst out into a great fit of laughter, and immediately got her speech and hearing back.

20. Her father was overjoyed, and kept his promise by marrying her to Lazy Jack, who was thus made a rich gentleman. They lived in a large house, and Jack's mother lived with them in great happiness.

Exercises

1. Which best describes why Lazy Jack wanted a job at first?

   A. To make money to buy things for himself
   B. To prove that he wasn't lazy and help provide for his mom
   C. To impress the rich man's daughter
   D. To buy his mother nice things

2. Which best describes the change Jack makes in this story?

   A. He goes from being foolish to being smart
   B. He goes from being lazy to being hard working
   C. He goes from being happy with his mother to not liking his mother
   D. He goes from being married to being alone

3. Which best describes the kind of person Jack is at the end of the story?

   A. Lazy and foolish
   B. Lazy yet smart
   C. Hard working yet foolish
   D. Hard working and smart

4. Why does Jack get to marry the rich man's daughter?

   A. He sees how hard working Jack is
   B. He likes that Jack is funny
   C. The rich man made a promise that whoever made his daughter laugh could marry her; and Jack did
   D. The donkey was worth a lot of money so the rich man wanted Jack to marry his daughter

5. In the passage "Lazy Jack" Jack gets many jobs, but never brings home his pay. In your own words, describe why he never brings home his pay? Use 2 details from the text to support your answer.

6. What is one lesson that "Lazy Jack" could learn from this? Be sure to use at least 2 details from the text to support your answer.

ANSWER KEYS

VIDEO
EXPLANATIONS

ARGOPREP.COM

WEEK 1

Monday

Rumplestilskin
1: C
2: B
3: B
4: B
5: D
6: C

Wednesday

Autobiography of a monkey
1: C
2: C
3: C
4: D
5: B
6: C

Friday

Red badge
1: B
2: C
3: B
4: C
5: Should include: She finally accepts that her son is joining the army
6: Should include: The story is about a boy who enlists in the army and at first his mother is upset but eventually she supports his decision

WEEK 2

Monday

North Wind
1: C
2: B
3: C
4: A
5: D

6: A

Wednesday

Cotton Gin
1: B
2: C
3: A
4: D
5: B
6: C

Friday

Gettysburg
1: A
2: B
3: D
4: B
5: Should include: It kept the south or confederates from gaining more ground on the union or kept them from winning the war, the union was losing a lot of battles and this helped turn around the war
6: Should include:Lincoln did not prepare as much as Everett did, Lincoln's speech was much shorter than Everett's, Lincoln's was more popular/ people liked it more

WEEK 3

Monday

Camel Hump-story
1: C
2: C
3: A
4: C
5: C
6: C

Wednesday

Camel Hump- poem

1: B

2: C
3: D
4: D
5: B
6: B

Friday

Aladdin
1: C
2: B
3: C
4: D
5: Should include: He gets it by tricking the princess, he tricks her by trading lamps, he traded her a new lamp for her old one
6: Should include: He loses it at first when Aladdin won't give it to him and he slams the trap door shut, he loses it when the princess tricks him, she tricks him by using a sleeping potion on him

WEEK 4

Monday

Law of the jungle

1: A
2: B
3: C
4: C
5: C
6: C

Wednesday

How elephants drink
1: D
2: C
3: B
4: B
5: B
6: A

Friday

Benjamin bunny

1: C
2: A
3: A
4: C
5: Should include: He was angry because someone was in his garden messing things up, because the cat was locked in the greenhouse, because things were missing from the garden
6: Should include: They take back Peter's clothes, a lettuce leaf, and onions

WEEK 5

Monday

Selfish giant
1: B
2: D
3: A
4: D
5: C
6: C

Wednesday

Emperor's new suit
1: B
2: C
3: B
4: C
5: B
6: B

Friday

Johnstown flood - a boy's heroic deeds
1: C
2: B
3: D
4: C
5: Should include: The flood was caused by a lot of rain, the dam breaking, and the rivers and creeks overflowing

6: Should include: Charlie is either brave, strong, smart or any of the like with details that match his character type

WEEK 6

Monday

Dan. the Newsboy
1: B
2: D
3: C
4: C
5: D
6: C

Wednesday

Queen margaret and the robbers
1: A
2: B
3: C
4: C
5: A
C

Friday

Wild dogs
1: B
2: B
3: B
4: A
5: Should include: They are similar because,some of them hunt in packs some live in communities, some live in forests
6: Should include: The hunt in packs, they hunt by tricking their prey close to their dens (homes), and they hunt bigger animals

WEEK 7

Monday

The Landlord's Mistake

1: B
2: C
3: B
4: A
5: C
6: C

Wednesday

The whisperers
1: B
2: B
3: B
4: C
5: B
6: D

Friday

The first English Colony in America
1: B
2: D
3: B
4: B
5: Should include: He doesn't kill him at first because of the compass, then he doesn't kill him because Pocahontas convinces them to spare him
6: Should include: Some things that went wrong; a storm stopped them from going to their planned destination, the captain was kidnapped, supplies ran out, disease and fighting killed many people

WEEK 8

Monday

Daniel's Indian Friend
1: B
2: B
3: D
4: C
5: C

6: A

Wednesday

Saving the Birds

1: B

2: B

3: A

4: D

5: C

6: C

Friday

Saved by a Dolphin

1: C

2: A

3: C

4: D

5: Should include: He survives because he plays a song and the dolphin hears it and the dolphin saves him because he likes the music or he was saved by a ship name The Dolphin

6: Should include: One version says he was saved by an actual dolphin the other version says he was saved by a ship named

WEEK 9

Monday

The Paddle-Wheel Boat

1: C

2: A

3: C

4: B

5: B

6: D

Wednesday

Why he Carried the Turkey

1: B

2: B

3: A

4: C

5: C

6: C

Friday

The Ice Age

1: D

2: B

3: C

4: B

5: Should include: Man learned to build homes from animals and he learned to save food from the animals

6: Should include:Things that changed; man used to lived in caves then in homes, poor flint ax was improved to polished flint tools and weapons and he didn't save food in the past but then he did

WEEK 10

Monday

Midnight Ride

1: B

2: D

3: D

4: B

5: D

6: B

Wednesday

Little Women

1: B

2: B

3: B

4: A

5: B

6: C

Friday

Why the Crocodile has a wide mouth

1: B

2: B

3: C

4: B

5: Should include: He has an open mouth because he dragged the boy to the bottom and then he wouldn't open his mouth for the goddess so she forced it open with magic

6: Should include: She saved him by putting her hand on his head and whispering magic to him. She made him forget anything ever happened

WEEK 11

Monday

The story of the picture on the vase

1: C

2: A

3: B

4: B

5: C

6: C

Wednesday

How flax was given to man

1: C

2: C

3: C

4: C

5: B

6: C

Friday

Ancient Man

1: B

2: C

3: D

4: B

5: Should include: Man survives the cold by trapping the bear and using his fur to keep warm

6: Should include: The effects are people dying, people moving, and man hunting new animals like the bear

WEEK 12

Monday

Land of the living and the land of the dead

1: B
2: D
3: C
4: C
5: B
6: A

Wednesday

How Raven helped Man

1: B
2: B
3: A
4: C
5: B
6: C

Friday

The making of a state

1: C
2: B
3: A
4: B
5: Should include: Advantages include; no more crime, protection, and it gave weaker members of a tribe a better chance to survive
6: Should include: In a state you need people, laws and leaders

WEEK 13

Monday

Greek self government

1: A

2: D
3: B
4: D
5: A
6: B

Wednesday

Why the woodpecker's head is red

1: B
1: C
3: D
4: B
5: C
6: B

Friday

Wizard of Oz

1: B
2: C
3: A
4: B
5: Should include: She is a brave or calm person
6: Should include: The house rises up, Toto falls through the trapdoor, Dorothy saves him, they both lay down

WEEK 14

Monday

Caesar

1: B
2: A
3: D
4: B
5: B
6: A

Wednesday

Tiger Brahman Jackal

1: B
2: A
3: D
4: B

5: B
6: B

Friday

Rabbit Lost His Tail

1: B
2: B
3: A
4: C
5: Should include: He trades his tail, a knife, a basket and in the end he got lettuce
6: Should include: The rabbit is a kind and wise person

WEEK 15

Monday

Prince learned to read

1: B
2: C
3: B
4: C
5: D
6: B

Wednesday

Indian never shoots pigeons

1: C
2: C
3: C
4: C
5: C
6: B

Friday

Little Shooter lost his luck

1: B
2: B
3: B
4: A
5: Should include: The effects are; he doesn't become a good hunter, he is sad, and he learned a lesson

6: Should include: The little man's bow and arrow is better because they always bring back food, he would have been called "he who shoots into the sky" and his arrows are worth more or better

WEEK 16

Monday
Spider and the fly
1: C
2: B
3: C
4: A
5: C
6: A

Wednesday
Hasty charlie
1: A
2: B
3: C
4: A
5: D
6: C

Friday
Be just before generous
1: C
2: C
3: C
4: A
5: Should include: She shouldn't have given the hat away because it was a gift from her mother, and you shouldn't give things away that aren't yours
6: Should include: Katie's mom is wise and understanding

WEEK 17

Monday

Tinkers van
1: A
2: B
3: B
4: C
5: B
6: B

Wednesday
Colonial People
1: C
2: A
3: D
4: C
5: C

Friday
Daniel Webster
1: C
2: B
3: C
4: B
5: Should include: Idle means lazy. He proves he isn't idle by memorizing books, worked hard at lessons and got fast in school
6: Should include: He is motivated to learn when he is called idle to prove he isn't and he is motivated to make money as a teacher to go to law school

WEEK 18

Monday
Swallows tail is forked
1: B
2: A
3: C
4: D
5: B

Wednesday
Parrot repeats
1: B

2: B
3: D
4: A
5: B
6: B

Friday
Polar Bear
1: B
2: B
3: C
4: B
5: Should include: The polar bear has sharp claws a long neck and thick warm fur that is white for camouflage that is good for hunting
6: Should include: The main idea of the passage is that a polar bear's body has many things that help it hunt and survive

WEEK 19

Monday
Virginia Wife Market
1: C
2: A
3: B
4: D
5: C
6: B

Wednesday
Charlie's Word
1: C
2: C
3: D
4: B
5: B
6: B

Friday
How the Iroquois give thanks
1: C

2: B
3: B
4: C
5: Should include: The maple feast celebrates when the sap comes from the trees,the strawberry beast celebrates when the strawberry ripens and the Harvest Moon thanksgiving feast for corn and many other crops
6: Should include: The harvest moon thanksgiving feast is the most important because it is for the most crops and lasts the longest

WEEK 20

Monday

The story of a great story
1: D
2: B
3: C
4: C
5: C
6: C

Wednesday

Britain before it was Britian
1: A
2: C
3: C
4: B
5: C
6: A

Friday

Lazy Jack
1: B
2: B
3: C
4: C
5: Should include: He never brings home his pay because he loses it by listening to past advice

and not thinking it through
6: Should include: Jack could learn to listen to advice and think things through, not all advice applies to all situations

ARGOPREP
COMMON CORE

Made in the USA
Lexington, KY
11 March 2019